AN EAST END FAREWELL

Stan Cribb begins work aged just fourteen when, much to the reluctance of his father, he joins the family business as an apprentice undertaker. The young Stan is soon burying victims of London's Blitz. His fascinating and at times hilarious memoir describes the East End way of death during the Second World War and the years after, when horses worked in partnership with their owners and funeral rites hadn't changed much since Victorian times. Stan takes us through the ups and downs of the trade, with all its quirks and characters, and gives us a tour that is both memorable and moving.

AN EAST END FAREWELL

AN EAST END FAREWELL

by

Yvette Venables

Magna Large Print Books
Long Preston, North Yorkshire,
BD23 4ND, England.

British Library Cataloguing in Publication Data.

Venables, Yvette
    An East End farewell.

    A catalogue record of this book is
    available from the British Library

    ISBN   978-0-7505-4187-9

First published in Great Britain by
Simon & Schuster UK Ltd., 2015

Published in Large Print 2016 by arrangement with
Simon & Schuster UK Ltd.

Magna Large Print is an imprint of Library Magna Books Ltd.

Printed and bound in Great Britain by
T.J. (International) Ltd., Cornwall, PL28 8RW

With your mane unhogged and flowing,
And your curious way of going,
And that businesslike black crimping of your tail,
E'en with Beauty on your back, Sir,
Pacing as a lady's hack, Sir,
What wonder when I meet you I turn pale?

From the poem 'The Undertaker's Horse'
by Rudyard Kipling

To Dolly and Terry,
my mum and husband.

Some people are lucky to find one
inspirational person to help them
through life ... I had two.

Experience: that most brutal of teachers. But you learn, my God do you learn.

C.S. Lewis
(written after the death of his wife Joy)

Death is more universal than life; everyone dies but sadly not everyone lives.

A. Sachs

Contents

1

The Apprentice
1942 (age 14)

It always started with a low moan that rapidly turned into a wail: 'a wailing banshee' our Prime Minister Winston Churchill used to call the air-raid siren; to us East Enders, she was 'Moaning Minnie'.

The bombers were returning for another go.

'Pull up ... pull up!' Uncle Tom shouted. 'Go and find a shelter, Stan, go on ... hurry up now, boy.'

I jumped down and ran along the row of houses, looking for one with a white 'S' painted on the wall, which signified there was a shelter for anyone caught in a raid. I found one a little way down the road and knocked hard on the door.

It was opened by an elderly lady with no teeth and a tea cosy on her head. All of a sudden my breath was taken away by a powerful waft of mothballs. I hated that smell and, to make matters worse, it was clashing sickeningly with 'Evening in Paris', a scent every woman wore because, I suppose, it was the only one around at the time. Both reminded me of great-aunts wearing bright-red lipstick with whiskers on their chins, trying to kiss me under the mistletoe at Christmas, but this heady mixture made me feel slightly queasy.

'Cor blimey, you're done up for a Monday, ain'tcha?' she said, giving me a toothless grin.

'In you come, love, quickly now, they'll be 'ere soon.' She opened the door wider, engulfing me again. Honestly, it was a good job I'd left my gas mask at home otherwise I would've been seriously tempted to put it on. She pointed into the hallway. I must have been staring at the tea cosy, which was knitted in claret and blue, the colours of West Ham United Football Club. It was securely pulled down on her head, and it seemed to have been strategically placed so her ears peeked out of the spout and handle holes.

Her hand automatically shot up to touch it. 'Oh, don't take any notice of this, son, it's me lucky 'at, makes me feel safe. Forget I've got it on these days, as I 'ardly take it off,' she chuckled. 'And me teef ... in case you're wondering, are in a tin can under the stairs. You see, I always take 'em out when there's a raid on, as I've 'eard...' she leant forward, lowering her voice to a whisper, '...that if you get 'it, the force of the blast can blow 'em out of your mouth and kill the poor

16

bugger sitting opposite.' She said it in a way that told me she'd only heard this bit of gossip in the last few days and was excited to be forwarding her new-found knowledge onto me.

I wanted to tell her that if she was hit then having her teeth in or out really wouldn't make a blind bit of difference – but I didn't. I swear to you, her logic was completely lost on me.

'Go on now, off you go, son, get down in the shelter.'

'That's very kind, ma'am, but it's not just me ... it's them too,' I said, pointing out into the street.

She peered around the door and gasped, 'Oh, my gawd!' She was staring at six magnificent jet-black Friesian horses, brushed so they shone in the summer sunshine; each pair pulled a carriage driven by a coachman, the first bearing the coffin, followed by two carrying the twelve mourners. 'Oh, my giddy aunt, you're a bleedin' undertaker. Why didn't ya say so!' she laughed. 'Go and fetch 'em in ... but 'urry now.'

With that I ran back and we started unloading the mourners. It was time-consuming, as most of them were elderly men and women and negotiating the carriage steps was tricky.

The sirens by then were screaming, and we could hear the distant drone of the bombers getting closer. 'Please, hurry up,' I heard myself saying. 'We haven't got much time.'

One of the gentlemen mourners turned to me, his face puce with anger, 'Bloody Jerries will 'ave to wait, son. They won't even let us bury our dead in peace. Dirty bastards!' he shouted, looking up at the sky as if they could hear him.

At last they were all off and heading towards the shelter. As the final mourner entered I started to follow when a booming voice came from behind me.

'Where the hell do you think you're going, boy?'

It was Uncle Tom, standing by the carriages, immaculate as always in his morning suit and top hat. He had such a commanding presence. He was around 5' 10" tall and very well-built. His head was virtually shaved, although there was a trace of white hair showing through. Everyone in those days had a moustache (not the women, of course!), but his was fabulous. A brush moustache they used to call them, and his was snow white. I always admired it.

'Er ... I'm going into the shelter, Uncle ... bombers are nearly here,' I said, feebly pointing upwards. I don't know why he was asking and not just following

'Exactly!' he bellowed.

Without a word of a lie, when he shouted you stood to attention; when it turned into a bellow you automatically cowed.

'They're coming, so *you* need to be *here*,' he said, pointing to the spot at the head of the cortège. I ran towards him feeling like one of those puppies who know they're going to be beaten, looking all hunched up ready for the blow.

'For heaven's sake, Stan, what's wrong with you, boy, you look like Uriah Heep. Straighten up. I'm not going to bloody hit you. Come on, now, stand here at their heads and don't you dare move! And for Christ's sake, don't let the horses see you're scared, 'cos they smell fear, you know.' And with that he marched off, disappearing into the house and leaving me alone with horses, carriages and coffin.

It now seems as good a time as any to introduce myself. My name is Stanley Harris, more commonly known as Stan Cribb of CRIBB & SONS, FUNERAL DIREC-TORS. It's 1942, I'm fourteen years old, and I am very proud to tell you that I'm an apprentice undertaker.

I was scared stiff as I stood there, not of the bombers flying overhead but of Uncle Tom. I knew as sure as eggs is eggs he wouldn't be in the shelter; he'd be lurking behind the tea cosy lady's lace curtains watching me, studying my every move. I could sense his eyes on me, and I'm deadly serious when I say that put the fear of God into me, not because I thought he would hit me, as he never did, but because of my job. I knew, being the perfectionist he was, one wrong move and I'd be out on my ear. I stood at the head of the cortège, as still as I could, holding onto the reins so tightly my fingernails cut into my palm. I wanted him to be proud of me. He and I knew there would be lots of lace-twitching down the street that day.

I looked around to check the horses; they stood grandly at the head of each carriage, occasionally scraping their hoofs on the ground or shaking their beautiful heads. One had left a pile of steaming dung behind it but it didn't matter, as I knew it wouldn't be there for long.

You know what, their calmness never ceased to amaze me, as our stables and garages were so close to the docks that on a good day you could read the names of the ships. That's where most of the heavy bombings took place, so they'd grown accustomed to the daily racket.

It was amazing how during the war animals and humans adjusted to the most horrible of situations.

Fortunately this raid didn't last for long. Normally we were bombed during the early evening or night-time, so having a daylight raid was unusual. It was over within half an hour and that glorious sound of the two minute 'all clear' siren was heard.

The front door opened and Uncle marched out followed by the mourners. I could hear the tea cosy lady being thanked by everyone.

As they left I heard 'Cooeee!' I turned around and there she was, standing waving at me. I wouldn't have minded if it had been a proper wave but it was one of those silly waves that Oliver Hardy used to do where he just kept moving his fat fingers up and down in front of his face. Then, and you won't believe this, she said all coyly, 'This is what I *normally* look like.' She stood there with her tea cosy removed and, I'm not joking, she was smiling at me showing a set of 'teef', which would've made one of our horses proud.

At that moment it did cross my mind that if they had hit you they definitely would've killed you!

I smiled and waved back. 'Lovely,' I said, blushing.

Uncle walked towards me grinning. He winked. 'You've got an admirer there, Stan. Perks of the job, son, perks of the job,' he said out of the corner of his mouth, as he carried on walking to the mourners' carriage to load everyone back on so we could continue onto the cemetery.

As we pulled away I heard a commotion behind us. Two ladies shot out of their adjoining houses. They moved so fast I

21

imagined they'd built giant catapults in their passages. Huge pieces of elastic attached to the surround of the front door which they sat in whilst the rest of the family hauled them back then launched them out into the road, their legs pumping like pistons to keep upright. Overalls on, hair tied up in head-scarves covering the indispensable rollers, both carrying metal buckets and shovels, they shouted at each other and were laughing. They pounced on the heap of dung and, by the expressions on their faces, I don't believe they could've been any happier if they'd found Errol Flynn (at that time he was the world's favourite handsome swashbuckling actor) lying there waiting for the kiss of life.

I remember thinking to myself, What has the world come to when shovelling up a heap of horse dung could bring so much pleasure? They shared it equally between them then ran back into their houses, no doubt heading towards their small back gardens where it would be quickly dug into their treasured vegetable patches. Then they could really get stuck into some serious gossiping over the garden fence.

Many people had allotments in those days. My dad loved his and spent most of his free time tending it. In fact, when the war started in 1939, due to the shortage of food caused by ships being attacked by enemy submarines, and cargo ships being deployed to carry war materials rather than food, we had an extreme shortage, so this is the reason why the government launched the rationing scheme.

All families were given a ration book, which you registered with your chosen shops. Each time you went in to buy food the items were crossed off the book by the shopkeeper. This made sure that people got an equal amount of food every week, as the government was worried that as food became scarcer, prices would rise and the poorer people would suffer and not be able to afford it. Also there was the risk that the wealthier families would hoard food, leaving it in even shorter supply. But the amount we were allocated was so small you could see why there weren't any fat people about. All we were allowed per person, per week was: 2oz (50g) butter, 8oz (225g) sugar, 2oz (50g) cheese, 4oz (100g) bacon and ham, 4oz (100g) margarine, 2-3 pints (1200-1800ml) milk, one fresh egg, one packet of dried eggs every 4 weeks, 2oz (50g) tea, meat to the value of one shilling and sixpence, which was about 1lb 3oz (525g), 1lb (450g) jam every two months and only 12oz (350g) sweets every four weeks.

Bread, fruit, vegetables and potatoes weren't rationed, so we tended to fill ourselves up with those, although fresh fruit was still hard to come by. We only had apples and pears when they were in season and, if we were *really* lucky, we found an orange in our Christmas stocking. It's astonishing how we coped with such meagre portions, but somehow we did; in fact, how we survived at all during those days was miraculous in itself. Nobody had even heard of the word obesity back then, let alone be suffering from it.

A 'Dig for Victory' campaign was launched and people all over the country were encouraged to use their gardens and every spare piece of land around them to grow food. Tennis courts, golf courses, parks and even the moat around the Tower of London were used to grow as many vegetables as possible. In 1943 the number of allotments had grown from 815,000 to 1,400,000. It was an unbelievable success.

At the end of the day, when we'd returned to the stables, I made us all a cup of tea and sat chatting with the coachmen.

'I couldn't believe Uncle Tom left *me* in charge of the cortège today,' I said smugly.

Jack, Tommy and Charlie were all highly respected professional coachmen. These men, all in their forties and fifties, had been employed by my grandfather and uncle for most of their working lives. They glanced around at one another, bursting into spontaneous laughter followed by all sorts of insulting comments, which I shan't repeat.

'What?' I said. I was seriously cheesed off.

'Listen, Stan,' said Jack, who was the Head Groom. We all looked at him stunned, as he certainly wouldn't be called 'a man of words' – he only spoke when he absolutely had to, and most of the time you were lucky to get a 'good morning' and 'good night' out of him. He had one of those hangdog faces, with rheumy eyes, you know the type – he looked like he'd never received one bit of good news in his entire life and was permanently on the verge of tears, but believe me he wasn't; tough as old boots he was.

'It's time you 'eard a few home truths. Now, just 'cos you're related to the boss, doesn't mean you're something special, you know. You silly little sod, if the truth be known we left ya 'cos you'd be surplus to requirements if we took a hit.'

As he got off his stool and turned to walk away, he stopped and looked back at me, leant over and put his finger under my chin and gently pushed up. 'Close your mouth, son, makes you look soft in the 'ead and you don't need any 'elp on that score! And you'd do well to remember *if* you plan on staying 'ere, respect's earned, not bloody inherited.' And with that he walked off home with Tommy and Charlie close behind in a state of shock at this unexpected speech.

I sat there for ages after they'd gone feeling

like an absolute idiot. What a stupid thing to have said. I'd only been an apprentice for a few months and although my dad hadn't *literally* said it, I knew for a fact that he wasn't too keen on me being an undertaker and now I was sitting there thinking perhaps he was right.

It all started in 1881, around 220 years after the first 'official' undertakers were recognised. The undertakers in those days were generally builders/carpenters who would be asked to make the coffins, so the natural progression was for them to organise the whole thing. My grandfather, Thomas Cribb, had opened the business with my grandmother, Caroline Susan, more commonly known as Carry. He started out as a coffin-maker for a company called Hannaford's in Canning Town. After learning the ropes he decided to take the plunge and open a business of his own. They had five children: Tom, George, Fred, Bert and Catherine, who was more commonly known as 'Kitty'. George, Fred and Bert joined them in the business during the early years, but George and Bert eventually left to pursue other careers, which left Fred – who was born virtually stone deaf – to remain as a coffin-maker. Tom wouldn't join the family business until 1934. He'd decided to go off and learn the trade in other parts of the country first. My grandfather died in 1925 and the business was run, until the day she died in 1944, by my grandma.

On 4 June 1923 at Trinity Church, Canning Town, their daughter Catherine married Police Constable Alfred John Harris and on 7 November 1928 I was born. Our first family home together was 25 Pulleyns Avenue and in 1930 we moved to 21 Ladysmith Avenue, both in East Ham, where I was later joined by two sisters: Olive in 1931 and Molly in 1940.

Every weekend we would visit our grandma's flat, which was above the Funeral Directors' shop at 120 Rathbone Street, Canning Town. When we arrived I would always make a beeline for the yard, not far away in Lansdowne Road, so I could watch the horses being groomed, the carriages polished and the coffins being made. Every time I walked through those large wooden double doors, with the small wicket door built into one side, I thought it was magical.

Over on the left-hand side were the tack room and stables, and at the bottom was the work room, where the wood for the coffins and carriages was stored. When you walked up the stairs to the next level, that was the workshop where the coffins were made.

Everything about it enthralled me, and as a boy I couldn't wait to grow up and be able to work there if my uncle and grandma let me. All my friends at school thought it weird

27

that I wanted to be an undertaker, and I suppose to others it did seem peculiar, but to me I couldn't imagine doing anything else. I know quite a few people used to call me a 'morbid little bugger' but it didn't bother me. I think I was originally drawn to it by the horses, as they always looked so beautiful.

My first recollections were from around the age of about five and a half, when I saw my first horse-drawn funeral leaving the yard. I can still see it to this day. It was bitterly cold and very gently snowing and I had my tongue out trying to catch the snow-flakes. My mum was holding my hand as we were walking towards the yard when the large doors opened and the cortège started to leave. She pulled me up. 'Put your tongue in, Stan, and stand still.' She then leant down and whispered in my ear: 'Take your cap off and bow your head as it passes.'

'Why, Mum?' I asked, looking up at her.

'It's respect, Stan. We're respecting the person who's died.'

I didn't know what she meant, but I did it – I took off my cap and bowed my head.

Everything about the scene was so spectacular it was as if I was in a film. The gleaming horses looked enormous to me. Their hooves made such a noise on the wet cobbles, and the highly polished carriages had a fine flurry of snow dancing around them. Then there was Uncle Tom with the coachmen looking impeccable in their overcoats and top hats.

I was captivated.

Even seeing the bodies fascinated me. I never once felt frightened. I don't know why; maybe it was because I was so young and didn't comprehend what was actually going on.

When I knew nobody was looking I would creep into the storage room where the bodies had been brought in and left on easels in 'shells' – these were coffins which were painted white inside and were used to fetch corpses from hospitals or homes before being prepared and placed into a 'proper' coffin. As I was so small I would have to drag a chair over to stand on. I would then gently slide the lid across and look at them for what seemed liked ages, but in reality was probably only a few minutes. I was strangely drawn to them, I think, by their stillness, as to me they somehow radiated an air of calm which I felt oddly at ease with.

When I was around seven, I was in the workshop watching Uncle and the other coffin-makers. This particular day was unusually quiet when, out of the blue, he looks at me and says: 'Would you like to make a coffin, Stan?'

I couldn't believe my ears! 'Honest?'

He smiled. 'Come on, I'll show you from

scratch. We'll just make a small one though.' He then proceeded to show me every detail; I can't tell you how amazing it was. When it was finished he even showed me how to French polish it. It was a day I'll never forget and it made me even more convinced it was what I wanted to do.

I don't know why, but Mum wasn't too thrilled when I returned with it under my arm to meet her at Grandma's, but she did let me take it home, as long as I agreed to keep it in my bedroom, which I happily did. But I knew it wouldn't be there for long, as now I had a coffin I obviously needed something to bury.

I generally got on well with my sister Olive, but she did get on my nerves sometimes. I mean, she couldn't help being a girl, but girls can be annoying creatures especially when they love dolls. I detested them, creepy things, with those staring glassy eyes and those little red lips.

'Peggy' was the doll's name; she would be carted around under Olive's arm virtually all day. Even at the dinner table it would be propped up and she'd make out to be feeding it. 'Open up, Peggy,' she'd say, with a spoonful of food. 'There's a good girl for Mummy.'

It seriously got on my wick.

This particular day, Mum had taken Olive out and Dad was at home looking after me, so I was left to play on my own.

The funeral was a very simple affair. Only one mourner attended. She was laid to rest in our small garden under an apple tree. I'd even made a top hat out of cardboard for the occasion. I would've got away with it too, if our neighbour hadn't been changing her bedroom curtains and grassed me up to Mum as soon as she put her key in the front door. I was literally dragged out by my ear, made to dig it up, and my lovely coffin disposed of. To cap it all I was sent to bed without any tea, even though I was famished by all that digging.

I didn't know what the fuss was about; I was only following the family tradition. I thought she would've been pleased but apparently she was mortified, as she knew without a shadow of doubt that all the neighbours would now be gossiping about 'her morbid little bugger' and how I was living up to my reputation.

This was all happening during the 1930s when people's lives were much simpler than they are now. Men were hard-working, women stayed at home with the children and life was basically good – very poor, but good.

As children we had a great time, running free, not a care in the world. Our parents were quite happy with us playing out in the streets until darkness fell; it would never occur to them or us that anything bad would befall us. At end of the day, all over the East End, voices could be heard calling their children in for their teas and we would sadly make our way home, dirty and exhausted.

But, like any child, there were a few things I couldn't stand. Sunday School, for one. It wasn't just me though, most of the children I knew felt the same. It was unfortunately compulsory for most of us, as we were forced to go by our parents. We were given stars to stick in a book, to show how many times we had attended; half the time we didn't go, so we cut out our own and stuck them in but nobody ever seemed to notice.

How would an adult not notice something like that? Life was a mystery.

Once your book was full you were given a 'special treat'. But in this instance the word 'treat' didn't mean what you might expect. It was a day trip to Loughton in Essex. Now I know what you're thinking: 'A day trip to the country ... now, doesn't that sound lovely?' But let me tell you, it was far from it.

The day started when we were put on an open-top bus at Swanscombe Street, Canning Town. We all made a dash to sit on top. It was survival of the fittest to secure a prime seat. Everyone loved to get onto the top deck and prayed for rain; it sounds daft but the reasoning behind it was each seat had these big leather capes, which were attached to the floor by your feet. You hoisted them up over your body and fixed them around your neck to protect you from the elements ... marvellous contraptions they were.

On arrival we were marched like soldiers to the Society Home. It was supposed to be an enjoyable day out but most of the time it felt like we were on military manoeuvres.

We then had lunch – although we called it dinner in those days. And what we now call dinner was called 'tea'. We were given these great big enamel jugs of lemonade, so big we could hardly lift them. This always annoyed me too. I mean, why would you give small children such enormous jugs? It was always left to us boys to lift and pour them out, and all the girls would be watching, sniggering behind their hands, just waiting for you to drop or spill it so they could then have a good laugh. I always thought girls had a nasty streak ... and they always proved me right.

But the point is, and I *know* it doesn't *sound* a big deal for an eight-year-old, but this was all very stressful. I always thought that things like that could scar a boy for life, but then I was lucky enough to meet Norman who changed my attitude to life, he really did.

Norman Floss was a new boy; he'd only arrived at Sunday School a few months before, and a funny little thing he was. Poor little bugger was pitiful, puny – thin as a rake, he was probably suffering from rickets or something. He was so pale he looked translucent and you could see little blue veins under his skin. If he hadn't had brown eyes you would've definitely taken him for an albino and, to cap it all, he had round metal-framed glasses with a big lump of sticky plaster over the right lens. Apparently it was because he had a lazy eye, but I never actually knew what that meant; all I know is when he took his glasses off his left eye dropped like a marble into the corner.

We were all sitting down at the long benches, eagerly waiting for lunch, as we were absolutely starving. The monitors came in and started putting the jugs of lemonade on the table. I couldn't believe it when they put one right in front of Norman. I mean, how stupid can you get! The poor devil looked as if lifting his knife and fork would be a struggle. You should've seen his face when that jug was put down; he was mortified, he knew he would have to lift it to share it out to the others, and that everyone was now watching him thinking the same thing: how on earth was he going to do it? I was sitting opposite him, a little way up the table next to Alan, my best friend, and we were watching him like hawks, continually digging each other in the ribs with our elbows waiting for the 'show' to begin.

Then the rolls were brought in and placed on the table and the monitor called out that the lemonade could be served. The sniggering had already started before Norman had even stood up. He put both of his hands around the handle. As he tried to lift it his little arms started to quiver and his face became red and distorted. All of a sudden I felt so sorry for him; I wanted to go around and help him out but I couldn't, as I knew it would only make it worse, so I just sat watching him struggle. Alan felt the same, as he'd stopped digging me in the ribs and was just staring at him; you could tell by his face he was willing Norman to lift it. He looked at me, shaking his head, then he leant over whispering in my ear: 'Poor little sod couldn't lift a scab off, he's got no bloody chance lifting that!'

He tried several times, holding it in different ways, but it didn't help; he couldn't even raise it an inch off the table, but do you know what he did? He stopped, looked around and did the 'strong man' pose, you know, arms lifted up at shoulder height, making out to flex his non-existent muscles. He then turns to the side and goes straight into 'Mr Atlas', shouting, 'Roll up, roll up, come and see the world-famous strong man ... the one and only ... Norman Floss!'

Well, everybody erupted with laughter, it

was *so* funny seeing this frail little boy acting like a strong man, but as I sat there joining in with the laughter, even though I was only eight I suddenly found myself in admiration of Norman Floss. He knew *exactly* what he was doing – by making people laugh, he was taking the micky out of himself, so we laughed at his antics and not at his physical weakness. It was an enlightening moment for me.

I told him afterwards that I thought it was great the way he'd handled himself and he just shrugged and said, 'My mum always told me "One of the greatest gifts a person can have is to make others laugh, Norman, and you have that gift, so use it whenever you can", so I do. I know I've always looked funny and probably always will, but I want people to laugh at what I do and say, not how I look,' he said seriously. From that day on nobody cared less how he looked, because he made them laugh.

When everybody started to dig in to the rolls, me and Alan reached into our pockets and brought out packets of sandwiches. You can imagine the stick we got from the others.

You see, the year before we'd arrived at the same centre, me and Alan were running around the building playing hide-and-seek, eagerly waiting for lunch to be served, when I happened to find a hiding place right outside the kitchen window. While I was waiting for him to find me I stood on an old crate and on tiptoes peered through the window. Inside was this woman, who was making up our lunch, and she was hideous. She needed a boil wash, there were stains all up the front of her apron, her hair thick with grease was falling down around her face, her fingernails were embedded with dirt and, to cap it all, she had a cigarette rammed in the corner of her mouth with a two-inch-long piece of ash precariously dangling from it.

As I watched, I was mesmerised by this piece of ash getting longer and longer, her eyes all screwed up as the smoke drifted into them.

Just then, Alan found me. I held my finger to my lips, grinning, pointed into the kitchen and signalled to the crate for him to climb onto. As we both looked in, this long line of ash fell off into a roll she'd just put the luncheon meat into.

She picked it up, blew on it and sent the ash scattering around so it landed on all the rolls below. Then, blow me down, she throws her fag-end on the ground, grinds it with her foot, reaches into her apron, pulls out another, lights that up, securing it firmly back into the corner of her mouth, and commences to close up the rolls – which she then starts piling onto plates waiting to be brought out to us.

By then me and Alan were giggling and nudging each other so much we fell off the crate, but we managed to get up and run off before we were found out. Needless to say we never ate a thing that day. When we got home ravenous that night, we told our mums and, from that day on, we were always given our own packed lunch to take with us wherever we went.

After lunch we were marched over to the forest into the glades and played cricket and rounders until three o'clock, then we were all piled back onto the bus to be taken home.

But I'll tell you what: every single time we came back from that place, we were 'cootie' – running alive with fleas and nits. It was dire.

Our parents dreaded us going but would never dream of complaining to the church, and I don't mean to be rude but it had such a bad reputation it was renamed 'Lousy Loughton'. But thank goodness they did clean their act up after the war.

The second thing that drove me mad was Friday nights. Friday night was bath and senna pod night. As soon as I got home from school, the bath was brought in from the garden. Some people had a big tin bath, a bungalow bath it was called, around 5ft long; others had a small one around 3ft long; some were lucky enough to have both, but we only had the small one. During the week the bath was also used for washing clothes and sheets. They were washed in the scullery – that's what we used to call the kitchen – then carried into the back garden to be run through the mangle. Wash day would normally last all day, and getting everything dry, especially during the winter, was an absolute nightmare, and that's not taking into consideration the ironing too. Then it was called a 'flat iron' and it had to be heated up on the stove, as there weren't any electric irons at this point. The saying 'a woman's work is never done' couldn't have been truer. It must have been awful to have been born a girl in those days.

In the warmer months the bath would be placed in the scullery but in the winter, as it was so cold in the house, it was put in front of the coal fire in the living room, which was the warmest room in the house – in fact the *only* room in the house which had any form of heating. During those bitterly cold months we would wake up to frost on the *inside* of our windows. I quite liked this, as I would stand and draw pictures on them with my finger.

Virtually everybody in those days had two rooms: a front room which was kept for best, when visitors called, Christmas or the laying out of the dead, and the living room where we spent all of our time and was located just off the scullery.

Filling the bath took absolutely ages, as the water had to be heated on the stove in a large metal bucket.

Once it was filled – and this is the part that always wound me up – Mum would bath first, followed by my sister, Olive, and *then* it was my turn. I mean, why did I always have to go last and have to sit in their rotten water? I was *never* allowed to go in first; I could never see why I would be dirtier than them. Dad was so lucky as he had it all to himself on a Sunday.

I often wished it was like the old days – and I mean the old days, back in the 1500s, not that I would've wanted to live then, but bath time seemed to be a lot better organised. Did you know they only bathed once a year in May – perfect!

The dad went first, followed by the sons, then the women and finally the children and last of all babies. Can you imagine the state of the water by then? It would've been as black as tar and probably as thick. You know the saying, 'throwing the baby out with the bath-water' – well that's where it came from.

In those days brides would get married in June, and as they'd already had their yearly bath a month before they'd really started to stink, so that's why the carrying of strongly perfumed flowers was adopted. Now, thank goodness, the bridal bouquet is only for decoration.

40

One day I piped up, complaining to Mum that it wasn't fair her and Olive always went first and had the benefit of the nice clean water. I said we should be allowed to take it in turns. I got worked up about it, shouting and being a right pain in the arse. I was a fool and should've known better, as it was always drummed into us to never answer back and to always respect our elders.

All she did was stand and glare at me. I hated that glare; I knew then I had pushed it too far. She then goes into the scullery and walks back in wielding a cane she'd bought at the corner shop to prop up something or other in the garden. She whacked me round the back of the legs with it so hard it snapped, and did it sting! As I heard it snap, I screamed, 'Don't 'it me, Mum, that 'urts. Stop … STOP!' I hoped it would make her feel bad, but she didn't take a blind bit of notice. She did stop though, not because I made her feel guilty but because her cane snapped. So what does she do? Only sends me over the road to get another one.

'Go on now, move yourself. Get over to Paines and tell him I need another cane because you've broken my other one. You can tell him how it was broken, too … tell him you've turned into a bloody monster who needed a good hiding … and I'm telling you something else: if you drop your aitches any more, my boy, you'll get another!'

She was always telling me: 'Stanley, don't drop your aitches and roll your "Rs".' I swear she wanted to turn me into Little Lord Fauntleroy. I would like to say that was the first and last time I got a good hiding, but regrettably I can't.

Right, back to bath time. At last it's my turn and at least I then get left in peace. I get undressed, leave my clothes on the chair by the fireside, and gently ease myself in. It's so small I feel like a contortionist. I often used to sit there fantasising that Harry Houdini must've come from a house with a tin bath and that's how he got into escapology. My knees are under my chin, my arms are hanging over the side, as there's no room inside, and, because the fire's roaring next to me, my arm – which is hanging over the side – starts to get really uncomfortable with the heat and takes on the appearance of 'corned-beef' – do you know what I mean?

So I'm now clutching a block of Sunlight soap, which was used for clothes, sheets, hair, body ... in fact, thinking about it, that's all you had; it was used for literally everything. It was yellow and half the size of a house brick.

I start to move around and try to soap myself but then I think, 'Well, it's easier if I stand up and do it and then sit down again to wash it off.' Now I'm not exaggerating – every week I did the same. I go to stand up and grab the sides of the bath to lever myself up and then I scream. I scream because I've grabbed the edge of the bath that has been facing the fire. It's like grabbing hold of a red-hot poker. Every week I did that and every week I would hear Mum's voice call out from the scullery: 'Oh, you haven't burnt yourself *again*, Stan, have you? You won't learn, will you?' followed by a stifled laugh.

Truthfully, if you were looking for sympathy you wouldn't have found it in my house.

Most people think of having a bath as a time for relaxation and contemplation; well, it wasn't in those days, it was misery. How I didn't develop a deep-vein thrombosis I don't know, and I always had the hump when I got out because I knew what was coming next.

There I was sitting on the settee next to Olive, looking all pink and scrubbed in our nice clean pyjamas, when Mum hands us both a small glass of liquid, which is our weekly dose of senna pods. This, in case you don't know, is a laxative. The pods were soaked in water and that's what we had to drink. It *completely* ruined your Saturday, as you couldn't leave the house; in fact you could barely leave the toilet. It was awful ... the devil's own brew, that's what it was.

I had a bitter hatred of the senna pod, as it ruined my childhood. I could never go to

Saturday morning pictures for years because of it.

People in those days were obsessed with their bowels. I never knew anything like it. All sorts of remedies and potions were taken, from Carter's Little Liver Pills, syrup of figs, Andrews Liver Salts to liquorice Pontefract cakes. I know it sounds peculiar but it was a very topical conversation in most families. The thought being that if you were 'regular' then nothing would ail you.

It was only when I started work that I had to insist I couldn't take it on a Friday night due to having to work the next morning, so I was then made to take it on Saturday night ... there was just no escape.

2

Black Saturday
1940 (age 12)

The afternoon of 7 September 1940 would always be known as 'Black Saturday', and was the day our lives changed forever.

The air-raid sounded around 5 p.m. and we hardy took any notice, as we'd been hearing them for nearly a year. Each time the planes flew over, we geared up for the bombs to start dropping but nothing ever happened. Little did we know that at first they were taking aerial photos of the docks and the surrounding area – reconnaissance they called it. All along, the bastards had been preparing themselves for this night.

I was in the garden on top of the chicken shed that me and my dad had just built for our twelve chickens. Nearly everybody kept animals of some sort back then: chickens, ducks and rabbits, some houses were like a menagerie; mostly they were kept for food. I loved looking after them and hoped that one day I would be able to keep my own. With our daily fry-up they were a necessity; the only other alternative was powdered egg, which was revolting.

As I stood there the sirens started, and within minutes I heard the steady drone of the engines heading our way; this time it sounded much louder than usual. As I looked up, my jaw dropped open; I couldn't comprehend what I was seeing ... there were *so* many planes. The sky for as far as you could see was filled with them. They looked and sounded like a gigantic swarm of bees. In fact there were around a thousand aircraft, which were sent to target London; they spanned twenty miles wide, filling 800 square miles of sky.

I leaped down, ran inside and excitedly told Mum and Dad.

'It's alright, Stan, take no notice, they're only flying over,' my dad said, smiling.

'But Dad, there's...'

'Calm down, you know this always happens. Just sit down and eat your tea. I've told you there's nothing to worry about,' he said, ruffling my hair.

I'd just sat down when an almighty explosion shook our house so hard I went flying across the room. I sat in the corner stunned. I was still clutching my bread and jam when Dad screamed: 'Quick! Under the stairs!'

We didn't have a shelter, as we hadn't needed one up to that point. Not one bomb or incendiary had been dropped, so most people squeezed into their stair cupboards when the siren went, but they soon got out again when they realised nothing was going to happen.

This all started the year before at 11.15 a.m. on 3 September 1939 when Neville Chamberlain, the then Prime Minster, had broadcast to the nation that, despite his long struggle to win peace '...this country is at war with Germany.' After that, within minutes, the air-raid sirens sounded and Londoners scurried to take shelter. As soon as the announcement had been made everybody was issued with small boxes containing gas masks. Adults had them on a shoulder strap whilst us children wore them around our necks. You were told to carry them at all times, which we did for a short while but then didn't bother and left them indoors. Street lights were turned off and we were instructed to cover up all windows at night with black-out material, so the German bombers would hopefully have an even harder time finding us. But since that day nothing had actually happened until this night. Hence it had been named the 'phoney war'.

But the 'phoney war' was now a reality. And this particular night turned out to be one of the longest nights of our lives.

The bombs started to drop.

Molly was only three months old and she screamed the entire time we were under the stairs. I remember thinking, She's only a baby but that scream! It's not normal. Babies cry and it's an annoying distinctive cry, but this ... it was horrible. It sounded like a scream of terror. It seemed to me as if in some inexplicable way she'd sensed what that night was to bring. I had to put my fingers in my ears to drown it out, as it made my blood run cold.

An hour later, thank God the 'all clear' was heard and we climbed out of the cupboard. I was so relieved it was over I felt like bursting into tears. We went outside and people were standing in the street, shocked and bewildered; there were some fires going on around us but nothing too bad.

Mum said to Dad that she wanted to go and see if Grandma and Tom were alright, so we went back inside and got our coats on. We were just about ready to head off when at 6.30 p.m. the sirens started again. We couldn't believe it! Olive now started crying, which nearly set me off, but we all headed back under the stairs.

The bombers were back with a vengeance. All you could hear and feel were explosions. They were bombarding us. It was relentless. I was twelve years old and I never knew what fear was until that night.

'Please, Lord, please, please, *please* let them run out of bombs soon,' I prayed silently. But they didn't.

We all sat quietly, as you were too frightened to talk. We just sat there waiting for one to drop on us. It was horrifying. Mum was holding Molly cradled in one arm who, thank goodness, had exhausted herself after the first barrage, and her other was around Olive, clutching her tightly. All I could hear was her saying over and over: 'Shh, it's OK, don't cry, we'll be alright.' I sat looking at them, wishing I was being cuddled too, but there wasn't room for me. Dad obviously noticed and put his arm around me. 'I know you're nearly twelve, son, and you may not need a cuddle but I do.'

I gratefully reached my arms around his waist and laid my head on his chest, as he put his other hand over my ear. I think he was trying to block out the noise, but it didn't help – it just made his heart pounding in my other ear seem even louder. I clung onto him wondering which was worse, the noise of the bombs or the sound of his petrified heart. We stayed like that the whole night, sitting in a tiny cupboard feeling that at any second one of those bombs would find us. It was continuous. Never stopping for a second – we were being blown to smithereens.

We were worried sick about Grandma and Uncle Tom living above the shop and, of course, our stables and garages, as we knew the docks were their main target.

We later discovered that the first set of

planes were the Luftwaffe, sent to drop incendiaries – a type of bomb that caught fire on impact. These blazes created 'beacons', which lit up a path for the heavy bombers to follow when night fell and, during that night, over 800 bombs had dropped in and around London.

The 'all clear' was heard at 5 a.m. and the overwhelming feelings of relief were inexpressible. We crawled out of the cupboard, so stiff and exhausted we were hardly able to stand. The entire East End had witnessed a night not one of them would be able to erase from their memories for the rest of their lives.

As we got out of the cupboard we grabbed our coats again. Mum put Molly in her pram and we left to go and check on Grandma and Tom. We didn't even get 100 yards down the road when we had to turn back. The ARP (Air Raid Precautions) and Rescue Services were all out, shouting for people to return to their homes.

People were wandering around in a complete state of shock. But the noise! It was overwhelming. People were shouting, screaming and crying, and fires were roaring all around us where gas pipes had been struck. It was incomprehensible what had happened. It felt as if walking through our front door had led us straight into the bowels of Hell. The flames and devastation around the surrounding area was a sight you could never forget. Some houses had been completely flattened whilst others were left still standing with their roofs gone and either their fronts or backs blasted out. Dogs, cats and chickens were running around bewildered, and everybody was completely disorientated. There was a horrible smell that filled your nostrils and we realised later it was the smell of burning flesh.

The further you looked up the Barking Road towards Rathbone the worse it got; it felt as if you were looking towards the end of the world. The sky had turned orange where so many fires were raging. After Mum saw what lay ahead she slowly turned away and started to cry. 'They're gone,' she said, collapsing into my dad's arms.

'You don't know that, love,' my dad said, holding her to him. 'I'm sure they'll be OK. Come on, let's go inside.'

We got back indoors and Mum was still sobbing; you just felt so hopeless. What could we do except sit there and wait for news. Dad decided that as we couldn't get to Canning Town he would make his way up to the Police Station – hopefully to see that it was still standing but also to find out any information.

We sat there for hours in a state of shock until there was a knock on the door. Mum jumped up to answer it. I knew by her face she was expecting the worst, but there at the door was Grandma and Uncle. Grandma still had her black bonnet tied under her chin, and was covered in dust but Uncle Tom's clothes were in a terrible state – in tatters. You could see by their faces they were severely traumatised.

They came in and sat together on the settee while Mum went to make them some tea. She'd started crying again, but they were now, thank goodness, tears of joy. When the tea was made, Grandma lifted the saucer off the table but couldn't hold it still and the teacup started violently rattling. She tried to stop it by putting her other hand around it but it didn't help, so she placed it back down again, tried again, then burst into tears. Mum took it from her; then put her arm around her. In all my life I'd never seen my grandma cry.

'It was so horrible, Kitty,' she sobbed. 'I've never felt so frightened in all my life. I honestly thought we would die at any minute ... how we didn't...'

'It's alright, Mum, you're safe now,' she said, putting her other arm around her, hugging her tightly.

We sat for a long time, all lost in our own thoughts. Uncle Tom broke the silence. In a voice so soft we had to lean forward to hear him, he began to describe what had happened. We thought our night had been horrendous but, to listen to what they had experienced, we couldn't believe our ears.

Shortly after the 'all clear' had sounded after the first bombardment, someone had started banging on the shop door. It turned out to be a young man who lived near the stables, panicking. He told Uncle Tom that three incendiaries had landed on the stable roof and that he could see smoke. Uncle ran back with him to the yard. They saw that the hay which had been stored in the roof had started to burn. They could hear the horses kicking their doors and whinnying. He unlocked the gates and dashed in. It was pandemonium; the ARP and neighbours ran in to help, and some were able to lead the horses out into the street. It was difficult as they were in such a state of panic and they were proving hard to handle. He said he'd never seen fear in their eyes before but it was there that night.

With their help they were eventually calmed down and the fires put out. Uncle Tom then managed to get them back into their stalls, only to hear the sirens start again. With that, he headed back to Grandma, leaving the stables unlocked in case somebody had to get the horses out again during the night. As he ran back, the bombs started to drop again. He saw people running for their lives to get into a shelter.

When he was nearly back at the shop a bomb exploded nearby. Shrapnel was bouncing along the road; he was literally flung up in the air with the force and crashed back down onto the pavement. As he started to get up he felt himself being dragged towards the blast. It was the aftershock of the explosion. The 'pull' was so powerful it felt as if his eyes were being sucked out of his head and his clothes were being stripped from him. He fought to get his breath; black smoke was all around him and it was as if the life was being ripped out of him. He'd never experienced such a terrifying sensation.

People were screaming, calling for loved ones; some had been badly injured by flying shrapnel, but Tom managed to get himself up and back to the shop where he and Grandma were to spend the most shocking night of their lives.

The bombing was terrifying for us, but for them it was a night of indescribable horror. With the perpetual noise and the intense vibrations of the bombs dropping so close, which made the ground move beneath them, he said, 'I truly felt as if I was going insane.'

When they left the shop the next morning they described the stuff of nightmares. Virtually everything was smashed to the ground for as far as you could see, across to the docks and the surrounding area. All of our immediate neighbours' premises, such as Wag Bennett, the bike shop, Parrots the Chemist,

Holmes the pawnbrokers and Wilson's all took direct hits, yet – and this is the unbelievable truth – the only thing left standing in that area was our shop.

After taking it all in and talking to the Rescue Services, ARP and also neighbours who had tragically lost their homes and livelihoods, they managed to make their way to the stables to check everything was in one piece and, thank goodness, it was. Like the shop, how it had survived was a miracle. The horses were badly shaken up but, amazingly, Jack had managed to make his way there and was taking care of them.

I'll tell you what was marvellous – in those days people just got up and went to work on days after the bombings. They might've got to their workplace to find it wasn't there anymore but they still made the effort to get up and go. Everybody tried to carry on as they normally would; it was astonishing. When you look back now, the spirit the people had made you proud to be a Londoner.

Winston Churchill got it absolutely right when he said this of the British people: *'They are a tough people, a robust people, who were able to bear home truths and make the consequent sacrifices.'*

The saying at the time was 'Keep Calm and Carry On' and we did ... but how we did, looking back, I genuinely don't know.

After we'd listened to Tom, we all sat there

quietly digesting what we'd heard when Grandma said in a voice barely a whisper – and I'll never forget her words – 'I feel as if God spared us last night so that the poor souls who were killed could have a proper send-off.'

As she said it, the hairs stood up on the back of my neck.

Neville Chamberlain resigned on 10 May 1940 to be succeeded by Winston Churchill. His first speech after becoming Prime Minister was:

'You ask, what is our aim? I can answer in one word: it is victory, victory at all costs, victory in spite of all terror, victory, however long and hard the road may be.'

It did prove to be a very long and incredibly hard road, as that night was to be the beginning of five years of inexplicable misery. These terrifying bombings continued virtually nightly for around eight months. During those first months, September into October, *every week* around 40,000 houses were destroyed, badly damaged or structurally damaged throughout Britain and, by the end of May 1941, 2.25 million people were homeless, and two-thirds of these were Londoners.

So many horrific stories were heard after that first night, but one in particular gave me nightmares for years.

Uncle came home the following evening and told us around 600 people who'd been made homeless the night before had been given temporary shelter in South Hallsville School in Agate Street, just around the corner from the stables. Entire families had been taken there and were waiting for coaches to take them away to the countryside, to safety. He told us how he'd popped in to see if he could lend a hand but was asked to leave shortly after by the authorities. But before he left he'd managed to see inside the school, and the sight distressed him so much he was relieved that he'd been sent away.

People were walking around in severe shock, some still caked in blood, faces black with soot and smoke, some hysterical, others dumbfounded, as they'd lost love ones or they were still missing. A lot of them still only wore nightclothes and staff walked around covering them up with blankets, handing out cups of tea, soup and sandwiches. A doctor was trying to help the injured, cleaning and bandaging wounds; many had badly burnt feet and hands. Others were just sitting silently in the hallways on what belongings they'd managed to grab, waiting for the coaches which they'd been told were coming at around 3 p.m.

But they didn't come.

He chatted to one of the fathers who'd been waiting with his wife and four children. He explained that the coaches hadn't turned up as expected but they were hopefully coming today. People were losing their patience and becoming angry. They just wanted to leave, as they all knew the bombers would soon be back; they'd even offered to start walking, just to get away, as they felt like sitting ducks in the exposed school, but were told to stay put and wait – so reluctantly they did.

But after a series of official blunders the coaches never did arrive. Nobody actually knew why they hadn't, as it was never explained.

That evening at 8 p.m. the 600 souls huddled together waiting to be taken to safety heard the sound of the sirens starting again and, shortly after, the distant drone of the bombers rapidly approaching. They didn't have to run to a shelter; the basement of the school was their shelter.

At 3.45 a.m. on the morning of 10 September they took a direct hit. Over 470 perished but the exact toll was never known.

Uncle discovered what had happened that morning when he went to the stables. The whole area was cordoned off, nobody was allowed to go near it, and press and photographs were banned, as the authorities didn't want the story to 'get out' and lower the morale of the city.

That night after dinner we sat around and listened to the wireless, but we didn't hear anything about the school. If Uncle hadn't witnessed it for himself we would never have known what had gone on. All the stories you heard afterwards were hearsay, and it was unnerving to know these tragic events were being covered up right on your doorstep on orders from the War Cabinet. This was done to prevent unrest and a propaganda triumph for Hitler, as it was later recognised as Britain's worst civilian tragedy of the Second World War.

When we all went to bed that night, I couldn't sleep thinking about all those poor people in the school, how petrified they must have been when they heard the sirens start.

I heard something downstairs; Uncle was sleeping in the armchair in our living room, as the shop was far too close to the docks to allow them to carry on staying there. I crept downstairs, pushing my feet into the crack between the wall and the stair to stop it creaking. Above the living-room door was a clear piece of glass, which allowed a bit more light into the room from the hallway. I put my foot onto the wooden handrail and levered myself up to peer through it. Uncle was sitting in the armchair. By the glow of the fire he was leaning forward with his head in his hands. I could hear him crying. I stood watching him for a few minutes, and I was taken aback. I'd already seen Grandma cry for the first time that week but to see him as well I knew I couldn't go in as he would have been ashamed to be discovered, so I gingerly put my feet down and crept back upstairs. I lay there for ages thinking of Grandma and Uncle – two people I'd never ever thought I would see crying. I don't know why, I suppose their characters were so strong I never imagined anything could bring them to tears. Ridiculous I know, but having lived through the previous four days and the unbelievable devastation which had suddenly hit us, I could appreciate how even the most hardened of characters would be filled with despair.

They never returned to live above the shop after that first night. Grandma moved in with us and, after a few weeks, Uncle went to live with his brother Bert and his wife in Leytonstone.

3

The Toilet Door
1940 (age 12)

People realised after that night that the bombings would be continuing for as long as the war was on. We couldn't keep using the stair cupboard for protection, so the local borough councils provided Anderson shelters to whoever wanted one to put in their back gardens. They were free to anybody who earned less than £250 per year; if you earned more than that you paid £7 for one. During the course of the war over three and a half million were erected.

They were made of galvanized corrugated steel panels, consisting of six curved panels bolted together at the top, three straight sheets on either side, and two more straight panels fixed to each end, one containing the door. They were 6ft (1.8m) high, 4' 6" (1.4m) wide and 6' 6" (2m) long. The council would normally erect them but we didn't want to wait, so I helped my dad build ours. Once built they had to be buried 4ft (1.2m) deep into the earth and covered with a minimum of 15" (0.4m) of soil. It always made me laugh that the government encouraged people to plant the top with vegetables and flowers to make them more attractive, and the local councils even held competitions for 'the best planted shelter'.

Because they were below ground the insides were damp and nothing could be left in them so, every night before we went to bed, Mum or Dad would leave a bag by the back door, containing blankets, candles and matches, a torch, rationing books and identity cards. This bag would be taken down with us as soon as the siren was heard.

Something else I discovered during the war was that even in the direst of circumstances we are still creatures of habit. I suspect most families were the same. After each air-raid – God willing – we would come out of the shelter still in one piece and head for the living room. The kettle would be put on for a large pot of tea and we would then sit around talking and listening to the wireless.

One day, only a few weeks after the bombings had actually started, Dad was getting himself ready to go to work for his nightshift, while the rest of us sat in the living room drinking tea. It was around 8 p.m. and we'd just we emerged from the shelter.

I never mentioned before what he actually did in the police. When he served in the First World War he was taught Morse code. When the war finished and he returned home to join the force they discovered he could use Morse, so they sent him on a course in order for him to perfect it. He was allocated the position of 'Wireless Operator'. In those days police officers in cars were unable to contact each other through radio. The operator, who was permanently positioned behind them on the back seat, would sit with earphones clamped to their heads, listening intently to any signals that came through from officers manning the Information Room on Victoria Embankment. They would be immediately deciphered and the operator would then instruct the officers sitting in the front as to what was going on and where, before heading off in pursuit of the criminals. He did this job throughout his entire police career. Even during the breaks for lunch and dinner he wouldn't be allowed to leave the vehicle, so he would have to eat in the car to make sure not one message was missed. During the war years he often heard the 'V' for Victory, beaten out in Morse over his radio ... three dots and a dash.

This was another campaign (we loved a campaign during the war) launched by the BBC in 1941. People were asked to show their support for the Allies by writing the letter 'V' in chalk wherever they could, and to beat it out in Morse whenever possible. It was also discovered that the first three bars of Beethoven's Fifth symphony echoed the

Morse code for 'Victory' so this became the call sign of all of the BBC's European wireless services.

Grandma, Mum, who was holding Molly and Olive, and Miss Thackeray – a friend of the family who'd been visiting at the time – were enjoying their tea and chat. I was sitting reading my comic when something strange started to happen. I looked up at the dresser in front of me, and the jugs and ornaments on the shelves started to move.

How peculiar, I thought. Nobody else seemed to have noticed but it wasn't long before particles of plaster began dropping from the ceiling like snow. Mum covered Molly's face with her shawl. I instinctively dived under the dining table.

'What's on earth's going on?' she said, looking down at me then up at the ceiling.

Within seconds there was an almighty *whoosh*. The entire contents of our chimney had shot out into our tiny living room, covering us all in a thick blanket of soot. Screaming, we jumped up and ran outside. Most of the street was out, looking stunned, but we were the only ones covered in soot. Mum handed Molly to Grandma and she ran back in, calling for Dad.

'I'm OK,' I heard him shout, 'but it's in a bit of a state up here.'

Debris had struck our roof, travelling

through to land on Mum and Dad's bed. Fortunately he wasn't having a lie-down, as he normally did at that time of the day, otherwise he would probably have been seriously injured, if not killed.

Most of the houses along our side of the road had been structurally damaged in some way, but across the road where my friend Joan lived (I say she was my friend, which she was, but I fancied her like mad) were in a far worse state. The damage had been caused by a landmine exploding in the middle of Kimberley Avenue, just up the road from us. The row of houses she lived in backed onto Kimberley; that's why they'd taken the worst hit, and thirty houses were completely destroyed.

Landmines were another of the problems we had to face during the bombings. These were mines that the Germans attached to a khaki-coloured silk parachute. They were pushed out of their planes and floated down to their target. If you weren't in a shelter and you saw them in the distance, you could never determine their final destination, as they'd be guided by the wind; a quick gust could blow them towards you or, if you were lucky, take them away. They caused huge devastation when they landed, as they blew outwards not upwards, flattening everything around them. They, together with the other array of bombs constantly bombarding us, were pure evil.

We then had the unenviable task of cleaning ourselves and the house of soot. A stiff brush was used on each of us in the garden to knock off as much as we could. Then buckets and buckets of water were used to wipe down the furniture and mop the floors. No carpets were on the floor in those days, only linoleum, which was hardwearing, waterproof and easily cleaned, which was a blessing in this instance.

Everybody was on the move after that. Houses were classified as uninhabitable. Luckily ours wasn't too bad, but it would still take quite a while to repair. Most of the people rented their properties, so when they were bombed out they would find another house or flat to rent. We were very fortunate to own ours, so for a year or so we rented a house at 12 Hall Road, E6 while it was being repaired. All repairs on the damaged houses were paid for by the government and classified as 'war damage'.

Joan's house, sadly, was too badly damaged for them to return to. It would be rebuilt but it would take a very long time. Her dad was a carpenter and he'd made some lovely things for the house, such as beautiful heavy wooden shutters, but they had been blown away into matchsticks by the force of the bomb; some of his furniture was salvageable though. They ended up moving to Eversleigh

Road, in East Ham. I missed seeing her every day, and we tried to meet up when we could. I was only twelve and she was four-teen but things were moving along. She was working then at the Curwen Press in Plais-tow. As I was still at school and she was out earning a wage she would pay for me when we went to the pictures ... it was all a bit em-barrassing, to be honest. But I knew I'd have to find money from somewhere, so I could treat her too, although once I got over the initial embarrassment of her paying, the prospect of being a 'kept boy' did have a cer-tain appeal. So after we were bombed out, I decided to use my initiative.

I was lying in bed one night and the idea hit me – I would make a hand-cart. I could help people move their belongings and make a few bob as I went along. All I needed to do now was put the plan into action. Firstly I needed a door and I knew where I'd find the perfect one.

The fronts of deserted houses were boarded up, so it was difficult to get in, but I went round the back of Kimberley Ave and found the house that had backed onto Joan's. I climbed over debris and a couple of broken fences and ended up in her old back garden. I headed towards the toilet – everybody's was outside then – and there it was, the toilet door, still standing and barely a mark on it. absolutely perfect! It was lovely; her dad had made it only a few months before. It was solid, made of oak, and I couldn't have wished for a better start to my new business venture. I took a screwdriver and hammer from my bag and got it off its hinges. It was heavy, but I managed, although carrying it back over the debris was a bit tricky. I had to drag it part of the way but once I got it out onto the street I slipped my old roller skates under each end and guided it home. As soon as I got it there I fixed two strong bits of wood underneath for handles and then painted it dark green. It was starting to take shape.

I couldn't wait to show Dad when he got home, and once he saw my endeavours he was so impressed.

'That's a beauty, Stan, where'd you get the door from?' he asked.

'Oh, I just found it lying on some debris,' I explained. I hoped he didn't see me blush.

'Well, I'm sure you'll get quite a few jobs with that son, well done! Just need a set of wheels now. In fact, I saw an old pram abandoned this morning when I was working it's on the corner of Gillett Avenue. If you go up there now, I'm sure it'll still be there – you can take the wheels off that.'

I didn't waste any time. I jumped on my bike and headed off. There was the pram, still sitting there, all battered with the hood hanging off, but the wheels were perfect.

Within an hour they were fixed onto the cart. I was almost ready to roll. All I needed was an old sack to secure underneath, as this was often used to put coal in when moving. With that done I was set for action.

Once the news got round that I had a cart, quite a number of old neighbours would knock and ask for my services. People used to load virtually their whole houses onto these carts. Mine wasn't big enough for these types of jobs but it was certainly big enough to carry bags and crates of personal possessions that people didn't want to risk being broken on the larger ones. It was hard work, but I made a nice bit of pocket money – certainly enough to impress Joan.

One night, when we were going for a ride on our bikes, her mum called me over.

'Stan, I know you've got your cart now. Well, we just heard today that we're definitely going to move to Denbigh Road in the next few weeks. Would you give us a hand?'

'Course I will, Mrs Davies, just tell me when and I'll be there.'

Two weeks later I wheeled her belongings from Eversleigh Road to Denbigh Road. As she walked alongside me she kept looking at the cart, touching it. I could feel sweat start to trickle down my forehead.

I thought I'd take her mind off it.

'So, are you looking forward to the move, Mrs Davies?' As I said it, my voice, which was in the process of breaking, went two octaves lower, and to my guilty ears it seemed even more obvious I was covering something up. I was so embarrassed, and thank goodness she didn't notice, but her hand kept sliding up and down the door edge. At that moment I'm sure she was thinking, *I definitely know this door from somewhere.*

I piped up again, coughing first, trying to get my voicebox under control.

'I was just saying, Mrs Davies, are you looking forward to your move?' Sweat was now dripping down my back.

'Mmm ... sorry, Stan, I was lost in my thoughts there for a minute. This is a *lovely* cart. It's so solid it's as if it was made by a proper carpenter.'

I cleared my throat again. 'Oh, do you think so? I hadn't noticed, but I suppose it does when you look at it. Tell you the truth I couldn't believe my luck when I found it just lying there on top of a pile of rubble.'

'Where did you find it, was it near you?'

'No, no nowhere near me; it was up by Nelson Street,' I explained with my head hanging down so she wouldn't look at me. I felt bad now, but there was no point in coming clean – what good would come of it? 'What the eye doesn't see' is what applied in that instance.

I had a marvellous time with that cart. I helped people move their possessions for years and made myself quite a few bob along the way. But little did I know my ingenious business plan would come back and haunt me several years later.

4

My First Day
1942 (age 14)

It was a lovely mid-summer's day, and I had
a feeling of euphoria as it was my last day at
Napier Road School in East Ham. I was
kicking a ball around the playground and
there was lots of screaming and shouting
from the other children when, all of a sudden, an eerie silence fell. As we looked up, a
gleaming hearse had pulled up outside the
school.

'Bloody 'ell, who's croaked?' said Alan. 'It's
not ol' tin knickers, is it?' he said, looking
around. We all started giggling. Ol' tin
knickers was our R.E. teacher – a very odd
woman whose ways were often a topic of
conversation between us. During our many
chats together, Alan, who always seemed to
be a fountain of knowledge about matters of
an adult nature, explained in hushed tones
that spinsterhood was unquestionably the
cause of her problems. Sounded like a lot of
old tripe to me, but I would nod and mutter
my agreement, although half the time I didn't
have the foggiest idea what he was on about.

'Shut it! He's my uncle and, take my word for it, you don't want to upset 'im ... er, him,' I whispered. Even then I was thinking about my 'aitches' – my mum's brainwashing technique was certainly working.

He got out of the hearse and stood at the railings. He was heading off to a funeral, so he was kitted out in his full attire. His eyes were searching the playground looking for me. I walked towards him.

'I hear it's your last day today, boy?' he said.

'That's right, Uncle,' I said, smiling.

'Your grandmother told me you still want to work in the business, is that right?'

'Yes.' I was now smiling even more.

'Right then, let's see what you're made of! Lansdowne Road eight o'clock sharp tomorrow morning,' he said, then turned around and walked back to the car. He climbed in and drove off without looking back.

I couldn't tell you how excited I was. I just couldn't wipe the smile off my face for the rest of the day.

'Now, son,' Dad said, taking another mouthful of his tea, 'are you absolutely sure this is what you want to do? Remember, you can't keep chopping and changing jobs. A job, *if* you're one of the lucky ones, is for life.'

'I know, Dad, that's why I'm so excited.

73

You know I've always wanted to join Uncle Tom, I've never even *thought* about doing anything else,' I said.

I knew I was bolting my tea, but couldn't seem to stop myself. It was the excitement; I had got the job of my dreams.

'Well, let's see how it goes, shall we,' he said quietly. 'You'll soon see if you're cut out for it. It's a hard business, Stan, not just physically but emotionally as well.'

What happened then had never before been witnessed in our house. Dad put down his knife and fork without finishing his tea. Mum placed her hand over his and gently squeezed it, then he looked at her and there was a brief glance of *something* between them. I'd no idea what it meant and I would never have dreamt of asking. I'd find out though, many years later.

I had a terrible night that night; I just couldn't get to sleep. When I got up Mum already had a cup of tea waiting and was going to cook me my regular fry-up but I couldn't face it, as I was so nervous about my first day. I was desperate to make a good impression, as I knew if I wasn't up to it I wouldn't have a job for long. Mum was worried that not having eaten breakfast I would collapse of starvation before I'd even got there, so a bread and dripping sandwich was wrapped up and pushed in my pocket.

'Got to keep your strength up, Stan,' she

said, pinching my cheek. Although she was the disciplinarian in our house, she was still lovely. My dad too was a wonderful man – very calm and quiet, he epitomised the word 'gentleman', because that's exactly what he was.

I jumped on my bike around 7 a.m. I had over a three-mile ride to Custom House. My life wouldn't have been worth living if I'd been late. As I previously told you, families were regularly seen loading up large hand-carts with all their possessions, pushing them along main roads looking for a new place to live. This morning wasn't any different, as I saw several families walking down the Barking Road with their heavy carts in search of a new home.

The father pushed it and, if they had an elder son, he would be pulling with the mother, whilst the smaller children followed behind. Every time I saw them it always made me feel sad because there they were, with everything they owned in the world, loaded up onto one cart. It just didn't seem right. After I rode past them I realised I'd been singing the old cockney song under my breath:

My ol' man said follow the van
And don't dilly-dally on the way
Off went the van, with me 'ome packed in it
I walked be'ind with me ol' cock linnet

75

But I dillied and dallied, dallied and dillied
Lost me way and don't know where to roam
And you can't trust a 'Special'
Like the old-time copper
When you can't find your way 'ome.

I sang it over and over while I pedalled and, soon enough, I could smell the stables up ahead. I was almost there.

'Good morning, Uncle,' I said happily, as I pushed my bike through the gates.

'Morning, Stan.' He was checking in a lorry full of timber that had just arrived, ready to be turned into coffins in our work room. It was always elm and oak, and it was brought to us in its raw form. A tree was felled and then cut into slices with the bark left on and then it was down to the carpenters to turn them into coffins. Even though I had a little knowledge of coffin-making, having watched the men as a small boy, and having helped Uncle make 'Peggy's', this was the 'real thing' and a skill that would take me well over a year to master.

'Oh, and before you get started, your grandmother wants you to pop in to see her on your way home, so don't forget!' he said.

'Right, come with me,' and we walked towards the stables. 'Jack?' he called, and Jack's hang-dog face appeared from one of the stalls.

'Over 'ere, Tom,' he said.

'Stan here, he's starting work today, so show him the ropes, will you. Start him at the bottom with the horses' hooves,' he said.

'Right you are,' said Jack. 'I'll sort 'im out. Follow me, Stan,' and off we walked to the shed. He reached up to the shelf and brought down a jar of jet-black oil, then picked out a narrow paintbrush and we walked back to the stables. He pulled up a small wooden stool and sat down next to one of the horses, then proceeded to paint its hoof with the oil so it gleamed.

'Once the 'orses 'ave been groomed and got ready, this is always the last job to be done, Stan.'

'Is it special oil, Jack?' I asked, peering into the jar, sniffing.

'Special oil?' he said. 'Oh yeah, it's *very special*, comes all the way from a well in Timbuktu. The well's so small only pygmies can get in,' he explained.

'NO! *Really?*' I could hardly get the words out quick enough I was so excited. 'Where's Timbuktu, Jack? And what's a pygmy?'

'You silly little sod,' he laughed. 'It's from the bleeding car over there, that's just 'ad its oil changed.'

He then finished painting the hoof, only how he got the job done I don't know, as he was laughing so much.

'There ya go. Nuffink to it, but make sure you don't get any oil on their skin 'cos it's a bugger to get off. You can finish 'em off later, as we've got a funeral this afternoon and we've gotta get 'em prepared first.' With that, he plonked the jar and paintbrush in my hand. 'You've only got twenty-three to go but make sure you give yerself enough time to do 'em!' And off he went, still laughing to himself. For the rest of the morning I kept hearing him chuckling in the stalls. It was *so* annoying!

We had six horses at that time: Baby, Stanley, Archie, Tommy, Tony and Prince. They were stallions. Everybody kept stallions for two reasons: one, they tended to be larger than the mares and have more of a 'presence' about them and two, because once they were castrated their beautiful jet-black colour would turn to brown during the summer months.

Jack proceeded to show me how to groom them and we got them ready for the afternoon, but it took me ages to paint the rest of their hooves, as they just wouldn't stand still. I think they were winding me up, as they knew it was my first day. Horses sense things like that, you know.

Our particular breed of horses were called Friesians and Rudyard Kipling called them a 'stud bred of ill-omen', and they were more commonly called 'undertakers' horses' but to me they were magnificent – I loved every single one of them and I know, for all their bravado, Uncle Tom, Jack, Tommy and Charlie loved them as much as I did. The other good thing was that you never needed to worry about them being pinched, as superstition said that they brought bad luck.

They had a naturally wavy mane and, when they were washed and brushed out, it left a lovely effect which – and I know this sounds daft – always reminded me of the beautiful actress Veronica Lake. You know the one, she had long thick wavy hair (although hers was blonde) which fell across one eye, but I didn't tell anyone, as I knew they'd laugh at me, and they certainly didn't need any more encouragement on that score.

You wouldn't believe the time it took to prepare them. We spent hours and hours grooming them until they shone. Over the coming months, Jack taught me every detail – from the grooming to the cleaning, polishing and fitting of the harnesses and velvets. The 'velvets' were around 4ft wide and 4ft long and hung down the sides of the horses. They were fitted onto the harnesses and I had to stand on a stool to reach them, as I wasn't tall enough otherwise.

They were exquisite; my grandmother had them made in the late 1920s. They were deep blue with satin inserts and edged at the bottom with a line of small tassels. On my regular visits when I was younger, she used to tell me how she would sit for hours during evenings cleaning every tassel individually. She'd then show me how to do it.

Although the roads were not as dirty as in her time, they still needed attention after a funeral had been held in the rain. It always took me ages to sponge them down and afterwards they were meticulously wrapped up and stored in a large old trunk.

It was mid-afternoon on my first day and we'd just about finished preparing the horses for the funeral when Tom came in.

'How's it going, Stan, you getting along OK?'

'Great, nearly done, just got Tommy's hooves to oil and then I'm finished,' I said confidently.

'Almost done are we?' he said, walking around the horse stalls, rubbing his enormous hands along their backs and down their legs, patting and talking to them softly – inspecting everything; let me tell you, he had eyes in the back of his head.

'Right, go and fetch a bucket of warm water off the stove ... now *warm* I said, not hot.'

'What do you want...?' I foolishly started to say.

'Don't you ever question me, boy!' he bellowed. 'If I tell you to get something or do something you bloody well do it!'

I swear even the horses cowered.

I ran off doing my Uriah Heep impersonation and brought back the bucket. He put his fingers in, testing the temperature. 'That's OK,' he said, 'now put a splash of that in it.' He was pointing to a tin of Jeyes disinfectant fluid. (Now, to my uncle, there were four things he swore by, Jeyes fluid being one. Then there was iodine, Armstrong's Influenza Mixture and block Saxo salt, and if none of them cured whatever it was that ailed you then I'm afraid you would, in his eyes, be classified as a 'goner'.)

You'll appreciate that I was petrified to ask why, so I placed a splash into the bucket and watched the water turn milky white. 'Now, pass me a piece of that there,' he said, pointing to a row of freshly cleaned hessian hanging on a line at the bottom of the stables. I ran and fetched it, then he took it from me and dipped it into the bucket and squeezed it out. He gently lifted the horse's tail and I stood aghast as he wiped its behind, then, after he'd finished, he replaced the tail and passed me the bucket and cloth.

'God gave you two hands to clean your arse, son; these poor buggers were only given feet – now get on with it!' And with that he turned and walked out.

It then dawned on me what he meant when he said I was going to start at the bottom.

On my way home that night, I went to see Grandma. She was sitting at her desk in the shop.

'Hello, Grandma,' I said smiling.

'Have you had a good day, Stan?' she asked, looking up from the books.

'I've *really* enjoyed myself.'

'Well I'm pleased to hear it. Look, I just wanted to let you know about your wages. I'm giving you 2/6 for the first month. I've started you on that, as I'm not sure if you'll be cut out for it. It's a hard business, Stan. You're so young and, during these times, with all the bombings and everything there'll be sights I'm not sure you'll be able cope with. But listen, if you do decide to stay then I'll put it up to ten shillings. How's that sound?' she asked, smiling.

'That sounds great, thank you.'

'Off you go then, son, your mum will be wondering where you've got to. I'll see you at home later for tea.'

I can't tell you how I felt riding home; it was as if I'd gone out that morning a boy and was riding back a man. I had no intention of packing it in – I just knew it was for me *and* I was going to get ten shillings a month!

I was already sorting out what I was going to do with my first set of wages. One of my plans obviously was to take Joan out, but my other was to take Mum and Olive to the pictures to see *Casablanca*. Everyone was talking about what a great film it was. It was being shown in the Old Grand cinema, more commonly known as the 'Flea Pit' along the Barking Road. The only problem with going there was that halfway through the film the lights would come on for the interval and an attendant would spray us all with a disinfectant mixture meant to kill off lice, fleas and any other germs that must've filled the place.

Honestly it was *so* belittling. I mean, obviously some people had fleas and lice but we certainly didn't. It crossed my mind too that instead of spraying us they should've filled up one of those crop-spraying planes they used in America and then headed straight for 'lousy Loughton'.

When I arrived at work the next morning my plans on how I was going to spend my wages were soon scuppered. Tom called me to one side: 'Stan, you need a black or dark-blue overcoat so you can walk next to the hearse, so buy one with your wages, and while you're at it you might want to buy yourself a razor as well.'

'But I don't shave,' I said, rubbing my chin, laughing.

'I can see that, you daft sod!' he said. 'Just get one and shave your top lip every day and it won't take long to get a bit of bum fluff going. In a couple of months I guarantee you'll have one just like me, 'cos if you want to walk with me in the cortège, you've got to start looking older, boy.'

I knew what he meant. I was a late developer and, as well as looking young facially, I was also still quite small.

Mum had already used up our clothing rations for that year so unfortunately I had to buy my own overcoat. So with two months' wages in my pocket I made my way to the second-hand shop on the corner of Thackeray Road and bought one for twelve shillings and a wallet for sixpence. I didn't have enough money for a razor too, that would have to wait until next month, so I secretly used my dad's. Mum was furious when she caught me, but when I explained the reason why, she laughed. 'That's typical of Tom. I should've guessed he'd be behind it,' she said.

After three months of shaving my top lip – sometimes twice a day – I would like to tell you I had a moustache that any RAF squadron leader would've been proud of, but I didn't. In fact, Miss Grimes, the spinster who owned the local cobblers, still sported a better one than I did. Gossip was that she was a hermaphrodite. I didn't have a clue what one of these was. I wanted to look it up in my dad's dictionary but I couldn't even spell it.

5

The Romford Road Baths
1944 (age 16)

It was during this time that V1 and V2 missiles started to be used. The 'V' stood for *'vergeltungswaffen'* translated as 'vengeance'. Hitler was upset that we'd bombed German civilians, even though he'd started the war and been blowing us to bits for the previous four years. But he was now panicking as he knew he was being cornered, so he set out to have these weapons created as his last attempt at winning the war.

The V1s (doodlebugs or buzz bombs, as we called them) were horrifying things, invented by German rocket scientist Robert Lusser.

They were in effect pilotless planes, and thousands of them were launched at London and the South East of England. As they flew over you would hear the ominous drone of the engine, then it would cut out and hurtle towards the ground. You didn't have any idea where they were going to drop. It was the silence that got to you once that engine cut out. It was terrifying. One minute you're sitting in the shelter with the noise above you and then … nothing, just ten seconds of deathly silence. That's the moment when people used to go to pieces.

Men and women would become so panic-stricken they'd be hysterical: 'Let me out, let me out! It's going to drop on us. I've got to get out!' they'd scream, fighting their way to the door, but they wouldn't be allowed to leave. Some would collapse while others would have to be physically restrained, as the fear had driven them to near insanity. They'd pull at their hair, screaming and wailing. It was too awful for words to witness people literally losing their minds in front of your very eyes.

Others sat praying out loud, most were silent, but everyone was petrified. There was nothing you could do but wait for the explosion. When it did land, and God willing not on you, you could hear people breathe again. If you heard another approaching in the distance you once more prayed it would fly over: *'Keep going keep going'* you would say under your breath and hope the appalling 'death drone' would fade into the distance, heading for some other poor buggers.

The blast from a V1 would extend across a radius of around 400-600 yards in each direction, and would destroy and cause damage to hundreds of houses. During the time they were used, they killed around 6,000 people and left nearly 18,000 seriously injured.

The Germans had also started firing V2 rockets. These monstrous things were invented by Hitler's favourite rocket scientist, Wernher von Braun. At least with the others there was some sort of warning, as the siren would sound and we could get into a shelter, but with these you had no warning at all, and shelters were useless against them. When they landed they made a crater ten feet deep and earth tremors could be felt a mile away. They were 46ft long, weighed 27,000lbs and broke the sound barrier, as they flew at speeds in excess of 3,500mph and could travel 500 miles. They destroyed with a massive explosion, followed seconds later by the sonic boom from the upper atmosphere. When these things landed they could destroy and damage 600 houses at a time. You could be sitting there minding your own business, eating your tea or at work, and the next minute without warning you would be blown to smithereens. I think most people believed these were the worst of the lot, as you had no idea when or where they would fall. Silent killers they were. Fortunately neither the V1 or V2s were used for very long, maybe just a few months, as a man called Michel Hollard – a French spy – located many of the construction sites where they were being manufactured, which enabled us to go in and blow the lot up. He was later to be called 'the man who saved London' and he received the Distinguished Service Order, one of Britain's highest honours.

We found out afterwards that even though these V2s were killing thousands of people, the incredible fact is that more died making them. They were built underground and thousands of people forced into slave labour died in horrific conditions. And the poor souls who did survive were hanged, burned alive or shot.

After the war, Herr Braun went to America and ended up working for NASA. His greatest achievement was that he led the development of the 'Saturn V' booster rocket that helped the Apollo spacecraft land on the moon in 1969.

Isn't it tragic, that from Herr Braun's and Robert Lusser's brilliant minds came the expertise for creating devices which caused incalculable deaths and devastation. I often used to wonder what these men thought of their weapons. Were they proud or ashamed?

This particular day I was left in the shop. Grandma wasn't in – don't forget she was in her eighties now and only came in three days a week. Uncle was conducting a funeral, so I was asked to stand in for the morning.

The door was opened around 11 a.m. by a

small, feeble-looking woman around twenty-five years old. She had two small children with her – a little boy around three and a toddler in a pushchair. She looked ashen, her eyes were swollen through crying, and you could see her hands trembling as she gripped the pushchair. She was having difficulty getting it into the shop, so I walked over to give her a hand. Unfortunately the way she looked was a common sight due to the fact that virtually all of the people that came in had lost a loved one through horrendous circumstances.

'Good morning, ma'am,' I said. 'Can I help you with that?'

'Yeah, fanks,' she replied.

We lifted the pushchair in and I took her over to a seat by the desk.

'Can I make you a cup of tea?' I asked.

'No, fanks very much, sir, I've got uvver jobs I need to do. I ain't got much time.' She looked at me with such sadness. The little boy sat on her lap with the toddler asleep next to her. She obviously had the weight of the world on her fragile shoulders.

I felt really embarrassed when she'd called me 'sir'. I mean, I was only sixteen and wasn't expecting it. Nobody had *ever* called me that.

'How can I help?' I said.

Taking out a handkerchief, she wiped her nose and said in barely a whisper: 'Me mum, dad and auntie was all killed the other night after a doodlebug raid. I'd been out, visitin' me friend, when the raid started and I 'ad t' find another shelter. When the all clear went, I made me way 'ome and ... I still can't believe it ... virtually all me street and the ones backin' on to us are gone!' She stopped talking and started to sob; her little boy looked at her, his eyes filling up. He quickly looked back at me as his lip started to quiver; his eyes were like saucers. I got up and, to be honest, I didn't know what I should do or say, as I'd never been in a situation like this before. 'I'll go and put the kettle on,' I said. I shot outside and filled the kettle. Taking a few deep breaths, I walked back in. Thankfully they seemed to have composed themselves.

'Have you found out what happened to them?' I said, as I sat back down.

'Yeah, they put a sign up in the street ... it said everyone that was found 'as been taken to Romford Road Swimming Baths. The Rescue Services ... they dug 'em out and took 'em there. I 'ate finking of 'em lying there in that 'orrible cold place. I just don't know what to do. You see, me 'usband's on the war front and I'm on me own now. We've got no clothes, nuffink.' She then burst into tears again.

'Look,' I said. 'You've enough to worry about. You tell me their names and we'll go over and collect them for you and then we'll sort it all out. Have you any other family or friends you can go to?'

'Yeah, I've got me 'usband's mum an' dad not far from 'ere. I went to see 'em earlier an' she said I can go there. Me father-in-law stopped me going t' the baths. They 'ad to be identified, see, but he went an' did it for me, thank the Lord. But I just can't believe it. Me 'ole family. If it weren't for these,' she said, looking at her children, 'I fink I'd do meself in, I really do.'

I leant over and took her hand. It was strange, I know, but it just seemed the natural thing to do. It felt funny holding a lady's hand. I'd never held one before, only my mum's and sisters', but that was years back. I mean, you don't get many young men of sixteen holding their mum's hands, do you? I'd been going out with Joan for a while, but going out then meant going to the pictures or riding your bikes together and obviously I'd held her hand in the back of the pictures, but this was different.

I looked at her. '*Please* don't say that. You're very lucky to have these two lovely children and they're relying on you to look after them, so you mustn't think like that. We can help you sort this out. Now give me what details you have and, as I said, we'll get everything sorted this afternoon.'

She looked at me; it was heartbreaking to

91

see her so devastated and the little boy looking so bewildered.

'Fank you, sir,' she said, blowing her nose. Their names are Elsie and Albert Fisher an' me Auntie is Florrie Parks an' the 'ouse was in Ravenscroft Road.' She then blew her nose again and wiped her eyes with the back of her hand. 'You said you'll go an' get 'em today, so when should I come back?'

'Come back tomorrow around two. My Uncle Tom Cribb will be here and he'll get things organised for the funerals. Is that OK?'

'Yeah, all right,' she said, standing up and heading towards the door. 'Fank you again, sir. I feel a little bit better now I've spoken to you. You've been very kind.' And with that I opened the door and helped her back out with the pushchair. As she went to leave she turned back. 'Oh, I forgot to say ... I went into the insurance people earlier an' they said that everything was in order an' they'd be paying for me funerals.'

'That's fine, don't worry, it'll all get sorted out, you just take care of these two,' I said, looking at the children. 'We'll see you tomorrow.' And off she walked, looking like she hardly had the strength to pick her feet off the floor.

Back in those days, everybody was organised and had an insurance policy to cover their funeral costs. Mothers would take them out every time a child was born into the family, as they would usually pay around a penny a week per person. It might sound odd, but mortality rates were very high back then and they always wanted to be sure that a 'good send-off' would be guaranteed.

Although people were incredibly poor they were also very proud and the thought of having a loved one buried in a 'public grave' (graves provided by the council for those too impoverished to pay for their own) would have been unthinkable.

When there was a death in the family the insurers would be informed and, generally, within a week the money for the funeral would be paid out without any aggravation. It was remarkable when you take into consideration the cost of living, wages etc. Pound for pound, funerals then were more expensive than they are today.

Tragically many families were to discover during those hard times that although mothers had been up-to-date with their children's and husband's insurance policies, if they died first it was quite common to find that the woman of the house had left herself off. This inevitably caused all sorts of problems for the family, who were left motherless at the same time as having to rustle up the money to pay for the burial. Some managed it but many, sadly, had to resort to burying their beloved mother in a 'public grave'.

I walked back into the shop, sat down and thought about what had just happened. Then my mind went back to thoughts of Dad and Grandma's words to me when I started: *'I don't know if you're cut out for this, Stan. It's a hard business especially during these times, physically as well as emotionally.'* Over the last two years I'd come to realise what they'd actually meant. Since I'd started my apprenticeship the war had been on and I'd seen sights which frankly I wished I hadn't. I don't know how I did it; doing a job from fourteen which even grown men were sickened by ... seeing things nobody should have to see.

As a very young boy everything had seemed so glamorous: the horses, carriages and clothes, even the bodies lying quietly and serenely in their coffins wrapped up in a white shroud. It never, ever, occurred to me how those bodies ended up being there or what kind of death some of them had endured, as I'd never witnessed that part of it. But now reality had arrived and my 'childish illusions' had been well and truly shattered.

I waited for Uncle Tom to return. He wouldn't be back for another couple of hours but I knew we had to get to the Romford Baths as soon as we could. Just the thought of it filled me with dread.

Many public baths around the country had been requisitioned into makeshift mortuaries since the war had started; the water was drained so the bodies could be placed in the pool area on tin trays.

After a night of bombing a fair number would be pulled out of the rubble and many of them were unable to be identified as family members, next of kin or friends were not around. Maybe the raid happened in the evening, when they were out; so when the siren was heard they would quickly make their way to the nearest shelter, but were then unable to get home until the 'all clear' sounded. It was only when they actually got home they'd discover what had happened – like the young woman who came to me so upset.

The Rescue Services would put a notice up stating where the bodies had been taken and then some poor soul would have to go along to the baths and have the unenviable task of identifying them.

A luggage tag was placed on their big toe with details of where they'd been found and the number of the ambulance that had taken them there. After the identification process they'd then make their way to an undertaker, give the details of the deceased, and we would then do the rest.

It was an abysmal job. The stench was so

strong it could be smelt from the road, but to go in there was indescribable. I dreaded being told that we had a body or bodies to collect from there.

One time we went to collect someone and a couple of undertakers from Surrey had pulled their hearse in behind us. We watched them go inside to look for the caretaker; they obviously hadn't experienced anything like it as, after a minute or so, they quickly walked out again then bent over retching into their handkerchiefs, which they had rammed up against their mouths and noses.

Uncle Tom walked over to them and stood talking. They told him they couldn't go back in, it was too horrifying, but they didn't know what they were going to do, as they couldn't return to Surrey without collecting the body.

He called me over to one side. 'These chaps here are scared to go in there, Stan, can you believe that?'

'Yes, Uncle, I can believe it!' I wanted to scream. 'Why can't you?'

But I didn't.

I didn't blame those men one bit; it couldn't get any worse than this.

'Look at them,' he continued. 'All burly and acting like sodding pansies. Let's show them how it's done, boy ... come on!'

With that he walks up to them. 'We'll go and fetch your body for you. Give us the coffin, their name, and what street they were from.'

With that, the men hurriedly lifted the coffin out of the hearse, gave us the details and, by the look of relief on their faces, I genuinely thought they were going to kiss us – they were so thankful that someone else was doing their dirty work for them.

We headed inside and, twenty minutes later, carried out the body.

The other dread we had after visiting the baths was that your clothes stank of death. It permeated into them. I've never known any other smell to do that, and once it was up your nose it stayed there for days afterwards, wafting up; it was sickening. When we took our suits off at the end of the day we would hang them in an outhouse all night hoping they'd get an airing. It did help, but that stench still wouldn't go away completely.

When Uncle returned to the shop, I told him about the young woman. 'Right, boy, we'd better get a move on then; time's getting on and we need to get them back here as soon as we can.'

With that, he picked up his bowler hat and placed it on his head – he never went anywhere without his bowler hat. Bowler hat for general day work and top hat for funerals; I never saw him without one or the other.

We got into the van and headed off. It was

now about 2.30 p.m. and still light. We only had about another hour or so of daylight as it was winter and the light was fading fast. The weather was awful – one of those dreary January nights, all murky and drizzly.

We pulled up and Uncle sent me in to check with the caretaker that it was OK for us to go in and collect the bodies. Everything was fine, so we unloaded one coffin and carried it into the baths. Just as we laid it down the air-raid siren started.

'Sodding hell, would you believe it!' Uncle shouted.

'You can stay 'ere with me, Mr Cribb, but we 'ave to go into the basement ... rules, you know,' the caretaker said.

'Alright, Mr Collins, it'll save us going out looking for a shelter. Come on, Stan.' And off he went following the caretaker with me right behind.

Just as we got down into the basement two or three bombs dropped simultaneously so close to us the building shook. At that precise moment all the lights went out – we were now in the pitch black.

'Oh, Christ!' the caretaker shouted. 'What do we do now?'

'Haven't you got a torch?' Uncle asked.

'No, I bleeding haven't. Left it at 'ome this morning. 'Ad a barney with the missus and left in a rush.' I couldn't see his face but you could tell by his voice he was furious.

We stood there for what seemed like an eternity, not knowing where to go or what to do, as we couldn't see a thing, but, as luck would have it, within thirty minutes the 'all clear' sounded. What a relief that was, but we were still in complete darkness.

Just then a light flickers and Uncle has pulled out his cigarette lighter. The caretaker looked as white as a sheet, his eyes were like organ stops and he was shaking like a leaf. I obviously didn't look much better, as Uncle held the flame up. 'Bloody 'ell, you both look like ghosts! You're a couple of nancies, I would've hated having either of you with me in the trenches. Well, come on, let's get moving!' And with that he turns and starts to climb the stairs. I was hanging onto the back of his jacket with the caretaker hanging onto mine, as we felt our way into the main mortuary area. As we got there the flame went out.

'Sod it! Burnt me thumb,' he yelped. I took it from him, lit it and turned to the caretaker. 'Thanks, Mr Collins, we'll come back tomorrow.'

Uncle turned to me and said, 'What you on about, boy? We're taking them now!'

Oh God, here we go again ... don't question the reasons why, just do it.

'I've got no idea 'ow you're going to do this, Mr Cribb, but I'll leave it to you to sort out. I'll be outside.' He then turned and started to feel his way along the wall to get to the main doors.

So there we were, left in the darkness with the awful stench, looking for three bodies. We had no idea where they were and we only had the aid of a cigarette lighter to find them.

It was unbelievably eerie in there. It gave me the creeps. When I told Uncle all he said was, 'Pull yourself together, boy, these here won't hurt you, it's the bastards outside you've got to worry about. Now, let's get down there and get on with it.'

As he said it I broke out into a cold sweat. I could feel it running down the sides of my face and back, and I wanted to scream: *'Please,* I need to get out of here. I'm scared!' but I couldn't. He never seemed to take into consideration the fact that I was still a boy.

My hand was shaking as I lit the lighter, this time putting my handkerchief against the roller to stop it getting too hot, and we edged our way down the steps into the pool area. I started lighting up the feet of the corpses, trying to read the names on the tags.

It was as if I was in some hideous nightmare, waiting to wake up screaming. Now and again I would have to put the flame out, as it was still burning my fingers even with the cloth on the lighter, and we would stand in the dark for a minute or so. As we stood there waiting, I could feel myself starting to panic. I suddenly felt claustrophobic; my breathing was becoming erratic ... I had to get out.

'Pull yourself together, calm down, you can do this, you can, you can,' I kept repeating to myself.

Out of the darkness a hand grabs my ankle in a vice-like grip. I screamed, and the echo bounced all around the baths. In fact, I have never screamed so loud and long in all my life. They must have heard me in the street; my heart was jumping out of my chest. I wanted to run, but fear had frozen me to the spot. I couldn't move. I quickly lit the lighter, but how I did so I don't know, as my hands were shaking uncontrollably, and there he was, still with his bowler hat on, crouching down by my leg, grinning. I remember it flashing through my mind that up until that moment I wasn't even aware he had teeth.

You know, he'd never been a man for jokes, but for some inexplicable reason he decided now was a good time to start. He scared the living daylights out of me! How I stopped myself calling him all the names under the sun I don't know, but without a shadow of a doubt if I had cheeked him I knew I would've ended up in one of those tin trays.

'Sorry boy, couldn't resist it!' he laughed. As he stood up he rubbed his hands together.

'Right, fun's over, let's get on with it, shall we!'

Fun, he says! I could hardly keep hold of the lighter my whole body was trembling so much, even my teeth were chattering. I didn't even have time to compose myself as he insisted we carry on. It seemed like an eternity. At each body we bent down to inspect the tags, and the smell, for some reason, seemed even more overpowering in the dark.

At last we found Elsie.

'Right, let's get her out and in the coffin. Stan, you take the head and I'll grab the feet.' Luckily she was all in one piece, so lifting her wasn't too bad. Some of the bodies we removed from there were in a dreadful condition. Many had been left unclaimed for days and days and decomposition had started causing flies and maggots to invade the body.

Once we got her out of the pool we put her in the coffin, which we'd left by the side. We lifted it onto our shoulders and carried it out. The caretaker was standing outside smoking a cigarette.

'All done are we?' he asked.

'Well, we've two more to go, Mr Collins, but as it's taken so long to find this one I think it's best if we come back in the morning when we have some daylight,' Uncle said.

I couldn't tell you how relieved I was. I just couldn't have gone back in there. It was one of the most frightening things I'd ever had to do, and to be honest I think Uncle Tom felt the same, but he would never have admitted it. As I said before, it was bad enough collecting a body in the daylight or when the lights were on, but in the complete darkness it was an experience I unfortunately would never forget.

The following day we left early and went to collect the other two. We took them back to the yard and Jack helped me prepare them for the funeral, undressing and washing them before wrapping them in a shroud.

I noticed another had just been brought in but this had already been prepared by a 'layer-out'. These were women who were called upon when there was a death in the family. A lot of streets had their own 'layer-out' and, as deaths would normally occur at home, someone in the family would be sent to fetch her. For around sixpence (£2 in today's money) she would prepare the body before we arrived but, more importantly, before rigor mortis set in.

Firstly she'd undress and wash it, then plug any orifices with wadding. Washing of the bodies was believed to cleanse the sweat of death, but also the sins of life; it was looked on as a form of absolution. They were then dressed in a white shroud and stockings, which every household kept 'ready for a death' in the bottom of a chest of drawers. In those days shrouds were always white, as white was a sign of purity and even writings from the 1600s relate to the reasons why it was used. In a poem called 'Death's Duel' by John Donne it reads: *Just as the body is shrouded in white linen so may be the soul.*

After dressing, a bandage would be placed under the chin and tied in a knot on top of the head, then pennies placed on the eyes as, when rigor mortis starts to set in – which can be between two to eight hours after death, depending on the temperature of the room (hotter rooms would encourage it to start quicker) – eyelids and facial muscles are the first to be affected. Superstition said that a corpse whose eyes refused to close was traditionally believed to foresee further deaths in the family, so closing the eyes was essential to preventing the omen from coming true.

Rigor is caused by a chemical change in the body. As the blood flow stops, the muscles form lactic acid, which initially goes soft but then becomes stiff and rigid. In Latin 'rigor' means stiff and 'mortis' is death. Once it has left the body, which is within thirty-six hours, the pennies could be removed. In Victorian burials, as well as placing them on the eyes one would also be put into the mouth. This superstition went back to 'Charon the Ferryman' from Greek mythology. They believed that the spirit had to pay him to take them across the River Styx. This river divided the world of the living from the world of the dead, and it was thought that if they couldn't pay the fee then their spirit would wander the shore for a hundred years.

After we'd finished and placed them in their coffins and put the lids on, it would have been normal practice for us to take them home and 'lay them out' in their front room, as we didn't have any embalming or Chapel of Rest, but in this instance the poor woman didn't have a home left, so they would stay with us until the funeral.

She arrived back at the shop that afternoon. Uncle saw her and explained that we had collected her relatives and that they were all ready for the funeral to be held. A date was arranged and they were laid to rest together in the City of London Cemetery.

I never saw the young woman again. She must have moved away to the country, as so many families did – either due to being bombed out or simply because they couldn't cope with the day-to-day anxiety of living in an area which carried the persistent fear of death.

6

The Encampment
1944 (age 16)

It was around March 1944, almost four years after that initial night of bombings, when the shop and stables were the only things left in the area. Everything around us had been flattened and cleared away, leaving acres of waste ground. One particular morning there was such a huge amount of activity going on, it seemed as if we were being invaded.

Army trucks full of soldiers and provisions were pulling up. It was bedlam outside, and the noise and upheaval was unbelievable. I went to see what was going on and was joined by Tom.

Lorries were unloading all sorts of things: tents, bedding, guns, food, everything was coming off them. As the soldiers unloaded they were being given orders as to what to do with it.

Uncle walked over to one of the higher-ranking officers and asked him what on earth was going on. The officer replied that the whole area was being turned into an army encampment until further notice.

This setting up of the camp lasted for at least a week; there were hundreds and hundreds of soldiers, not just English but Polish, Czechoslovakian and Norwegians. The area it covered was enormous, from where we were to all the way over in Silvertown. In fact it covered all of the surrounding area.

Fences were placed around it, with thick barbed wire fitted along the top and, instead of them working around our little shop and stables, they decided the best thing was to incorporate us into it. It was funny, because anybody coming in to see us would have to walk through gates and an armed sentry. We did have a laugh about being the only undertakers in England to have our own armed guards.

When I used to lock up at night the Military Police, who used to stand at the gates, would call out, 'Goodnight, young Cribb, see you in the morning.' It was great in a way; it certainly made you feel safe.

Although one day down at the stables Jack had been grooming the horses when a round of machine-gun fire blasted out, splintering the frame of the stable. He ducked for cover, thinking he was under attack. He could hear footsteps outside as the firing continued. He stayed cowering in the corner even after the firing had stopped, not knowing what he should do when half an hour later Uncle walked in.

'Am I glad to see you, Tom,' he said, creeping out from behind the stable.

'Why? What on earth's happened? You look scared to death!'

'Had a round of machine-gun fire come in 'ere and hit the wood on the corner of the stable where I was grooming Archie. Don't know how it missed us.'

With that he turns and goes to the door and looks carefully around outside. He walks closely along the side of the stables and around the corner he comes across a soldier with his face blackened up, lying on his stomach behind a pile of rubble.

'Did you just shoot a sodding round into my stables? You nearly shot my groom and horse!' he says furiously, looking at the man on the ground.

The soldier stands up. 'Bloody 'ell, sorry about that, guv, I didn't know the stables were still occupied. I thought they were empty! Nobody told me to avoid 'em, we're on commando training.'

'Who's your Officer in Charge, boy? I'll have to go and have a word with him. Can't have this, it's too sodding dangerous!'

When he found the officer and told him what had happened he was extremely apologetic and guaranteed it wouldn't happen again and, fortunately it didn't, but it turned out to be a very peculiar couple of months.

Although we'd asked the soldiers on several occasions what they were doing there, we never got a proper answer. They said it was a 'training camp', but it felt there was more to it than that.

One Friday towards the end of May, I'd gone into work as usual, but something in the encampment certainly wasn't normal. I couldn't put my finger on it; there was always plenty of activity but it seemed different somehow, the atmosphere had altered drastically, the soldiers were on edge and, as the week progressed, so did the anxiety levels – you could sense it.

When I got home that evening I told Mum and Dad how strange it was around the barracks, how everything seemed different, and how the normally friendly soldiers were abrupt and preoccupied.

After tea I went over to Joan's house. She was home for the weekend from her Land Army duties – but I'll tell you about that later. I suggested we go for a ride up to the Iron Bridge in Silvertown, as I wanted to watch what was going on. We occasionally rode down there and stood on the bridge, as it afforded us a great view over the camp and we would stand and watch the soldiers going about their duties.

That night there was a considerable amount of action going on. Everybody was being industrious. We couldn't make out what exactly they were doing, but whatever it was you could sense it was vital. We rode slowly back, side by side, discussing what we'd seen, and unable to come to any conclusions.

The following Monday I headed off back to the shop; we had an early start so I had to get in especially early to open up.

As I rode along the Barking Road the weirdest thing hit me; it was quiet, unnaturally quiet. I slowed my bike and gently pedalled along, but looking through the fence of the camp, I couldn't see anyone. That's odd, I thought, perhaps they're all over the other side at a meeting or something. But then I reached the shop. There was no sentry on the gates; in fact the gates were open. I got off my bike and pushed it in.

You know in those old cowboy films, when they ride into a deserted town and tumbleweed is blowing across the set, well that's *exactly* what it was like. I've never witnessed anything so eerie (except for the Romford Baths) in all my life, and that's saying something being an undertaker. Everyone and everything had gone – an entire encampment of soldiers, tanks and lorries vanished! I got back on my bike and rode up to the stables – it was the same: nothing, all gone. I just couldn't believe my eyes. Where on earth was everyone?

When Grandma, Uncle and the rest of the

staff turned up, we all stood outside looking at this once vibrant area that had disappeared overnight. None of us had any notion of what was happening.

That evening I was explaining it all to Mum and Dad again. Joan had gone back to her duties the day before, so she was unaware of the mysterious new developments. We sat around trying to work it out. Did they have 'inside information'? Were they expecting us to be attacked? Maybe all of Hitler's resources were going to be pointed at us and that's why they'd shifted. We were all desperately worried that we were going to be the target of one almighty raid.

We had a long, restless night; as you can imagine. But in the morning, thank goodness, we were all still in one piece. So it was work as normal. Our usual mid-morning cuppa was made and we sat chatting and listening to the wireless, when all of a sudden a voice broke in:

'This is the BBC Home Service and here is a special bulletin... D-Day has come. Early this morning the Allies began the assault on the north-western face of Hitler's European fortress. The first official news came just after half-past nine when Supreme Headquarters of the Allied Expeditionary Force issued communiqué Number One. This said: "Under the command of General Eisenhower Allied naval forces supported by strong air forces began landing Allied armies

this morning on the northern coast of France.'"

We sat there dumbfounded. We'd invaded Europe! I had goose-bumps all over. This was it! This now was the start of the beginning of the end. It was our last 'hurrah', as they used to say. If we failed now, England would be ruled by Germany. We *had* to succeed. It was the D-Day landings – the largest amphibious invasion of all time and, in fact, it did win us the war.

Although we invaded on the 6th, the actually invasion was originally set for the 5th June, but the weather was so bad it had been postponed. The month of May had been very nice weather-wise, so the raid had been set. But as we went into June it started to deteriorate and there were major debates between General Eisenhower and General Montgomery as to whether we'd be able to continue. The discussions took place right up to the line and the meteorologists were constantly checking the forecasts. Some wanted to cancel and re-schedule for a month ahead – it had to be a month ahead, as the date needed to be near or on a full moon so there was illumination. Everything and everyone, and I mean everyone – Army, Air Force and Navy – were all geared up for this one moment, so to cancel was not an option. Fortunately for us, the weather predicted for the 6th was slightly better, and the seas were meant to be calmer, so it was decided that the 6th would be the date. And it was. Around 156,000 men from Britain, Canada and the US were deployed on 'Operation Overlord' and it was to be one of the largest military invasions in world history.

The other fortunate factor for us was that the Germans were not expecting us. Due to the bad weather they never dreamt an invasion was imminent, so dozens of the regimental and battalion commanders were away from their posts. Even their man in charge, Field Marshal Rommel, took a few days off, as it was his wife's birthday. We caught them completely off guard.

So, now we knew this was the reason our encampment had been set up; it was in order to train the soldiers for the D-Day landings. The words of Irish journalist Cornelius Ryan describe the scope of this massive military action:

'They came, rank after relentless rank, ten lanes wide, twenty miles across, five thousand ships of every description. There were fast new attack transports, slow rust-scarred freighters, small ocean liners, Channel steamers, hospital ships, weather-beaten tankers, coasters and swarms of fussing tugs. There were endless columns of shal-low-draft landing ships – great wallowing vessels, some of them almost 350ft long... Ahead of the convoys were processions of mine sweepers, Coast Guard cutters, buoy-layers and motor launches. Barrage balloons flew above the ships. Squadrons

of fighter planes weaved below the clouds. And surrounding this fantastic cavalcade of ships packed with men, guns, tanks, motor vehicles and supplies ... was a formidable array of 702 war-ships.'

But what had become of the soldiers who had befriended us during those months? We hoped to goodness they'd survived, as we were later to discover that at least 12,000 men who had fought in those landings had been killed or wounded.

7

Our Wonderful Horses
1944 (age 16)

I had spent many evenings after work sitting nursing a cup of tea in the shop, listening to Uncle Tom talk about the business. I used to love those chats. We would sit opposite each other in front of our small open fire, with the glow of the embers in the grate. Now and again he would tell me to throw an off-cut of elm onto it, which was useless as firewood as it never actually burned – all it did was smoulder – and, if a sudden gust of wind blew down the chimney, we would end up being engulfed in smoke.

With his back to the window, the light from the street lamp shone behind him, turning him into a silhouette. All I could hear was his low, melodic voice relaying his younger days to me and I watched the glow of his Wood-bine as he paused to take the occasional puff.

I was spellbound.

He had spent a long time away from the family business working for a number of different funeral directors in the Surrey area, one being Frederick W Paine in Kingston.

These companies often dealt with the gentry and aristocracy, and he'd learnt so much from them. To me he was a visionary; he would explain what he believed the future held for the business – such as fridges in which to store bodies. Fridges! I'd never heard of one let alone seen one. He described a box which stayed cold and you would put milk, butter and meat into it to stop it from going off – I couldn't imagine such a thing let alone the idea of putting bodies into it. Embalming was another, and so the list went on. On one of these occasions he told me, 'Stan, the best advice I can give you is to treat every funeral as if it's your first. If you ever feel you're becoming complacent you must promise me that you'll leave and find another job. Complacency shouldn't be tolerated in any business, but being in this profession it's not only unacceptable it's unforgivable. People entrust their loved ones to us, they expect them to be treated with the utmost dignity and respect; this cannot be compromised in any shape or form and I will not tolerate it.'

As well as learning more about the trade with each passing month, time was catching up with another integral part of our daily lives. By the end of the month Archie, Baby and Stanley would be dead, and all of our beloved horses would be gone.

Baby was the eldest, and pulling the

carriages had become difficult for him, so we were working with only five. Odd numbers are not much good to an undertaker, as he needs a pair of horses to pull a carriage. So we made the decision to either buy another or get rid of the ones we had.

So the decision was made: the horses had to go, as Uncle knew that motor vehicles would soon be taking over and it wouldn't be long before the horse-drawn carriages would be obsolete.

It was devastating news. We all stood looking at one another not knowing what to say or do. Remember, those horses had been with us for ten years or more. I'd only worked with them for two years but had grown up with them around me. The men had worked with them every single day, and they were as much a part of us as we were to them. I swallowed hard. My eyes were welling up with tears.

'Right, we have two weeks before everything is taken to the horse repository for auction. I want everything cleaned, packed up and ready to go. I'm sorry, lads, but that's the way it is,' Tom said.

We all knew not to question his decision, so we didn't. We just got to work.

On the Sunday before the auction, which was being held on the Monday morning, we all met at the stables. Charlie and Tommy sorted the carriages. I started on the horses with Jack. I began with Tommy – my favourite. I loved them all but I'd learnt the ropes with him and he was a bit special to me. I was talking to him, as I always did, but this time my voice kept cracking. Normally he stood still when he was being groomed but today was different. He was nuzzling and pushing me with his nose. I truly believe he knew something was going on; it was the way he kept leaning into me. As I bent down and started on his legs, the tears that had been welling up just dropped down into the straw. I was finding it hard to stop them. I got my handkerchief out and wiped my eyes quickly so the others wouldn't see.

I was then left with Tony, who was also acting strangely. He was the opposite of Tommy – normally quite lively and enjoyed being brushed, but today he stood dead still with his head dropped. I kept trying to get him to lift it but he wouldn't. During that hour I have never felt such sorrow. Our beautiful horses were going and we would never see them again. We were heartbroken.

After they'd been groomed we harnessed them up to the three carriages and, without a word being spoken, drove them through London to the Elephant and Castle and left them at the repository. Although there was a war on this would be only the second time that I'd witnessed grown men cry. To this day I don't know how we walked away from them.

The following morning I was up at 4 a.m. I hadn't slept a wink all night; in fact, I cried for most of it. Mum heard me get up, so she got up too, wanting to cook me breakfast, but I just couldn't face it. I left carrying a paper bag of carrots and caught a No. 40 bus back to the Elephant and Castle to meet Jack. Uncle was coming later for the auction.

When Jack arrived we made our way to the horses. We'd arranged that we would groom them together for one last time to get them looking extra special for the auction. They whinnied when they saw us, as they always did, and my throat closed up and tears filled my eyes again. I could barely see.

'Let's get this done, Stan, let's make 'em shine one last time,' Jack said, stroking Archie. His voice had started to quiver, so he quickly looked away and began to brush him.

I thought the previous day had been hard, but now my heart felt as if it was literally going to break. I had a physical pain in my chest; I couldn't breathe. It was impossible to hold back the tears any longer.

'I'm sorry, Jack, I can't help it,' I said, burying my head into Tommy's neck as I sobbed.

'It's alright, son. I know,' is all he said, not looking around.

After we'd finished I went back to each

one, feeding them carrots whilst whispering how much I loved them and gave them one last hug.

We left them in their stalls and went outside to meet Tom, then waited for the auction to start. Within half an hour, Prince, Tony and Tommy had been sold and so had our hearse and two mourning carriages. We were stunned when my grandfather's original hearse, which he'd had specially commissioned in 1912 and had paid a king's ransom of £200 for, went for a mere £14. The only items we kept were our 'velvets', which were stored away in a trunk in our office.

Later on, our worst fears came true. Baby, Archie and Stanley were not sold, as they were deemed too old. That afternoon they were taken away to be destroyed.

How I wanted to save them!

I would have done anything *absolutely anything* to stop them being taken away. Without a word of a lie, if someone had walked up to me right then and said, 'If I cut your right arm off you can keep the horses,' I would have held it out, closed my eyes and said, 'Do it!' I really would have, but that didn't happen; in fact nothing happened. Uncle was adamant. 'I'm sorry boys, but there's nothing we can do,' he said, shaking his head.

Tears blinded our eyes as we watched them being led away. All their lives they had trusted us but now we had betrayed them –

our wonderful, loyal beautiful friends. Not only was it unbearable to see three of them sold, but for the others to be destroyed was beyond comprehension.

I would not work with horses again for another forty years.

It was around four months after the auction. I was getting ready to leave for work when Grandma called to me from upstairs.

'Stan, will you come up a minute, please?'

I ran up to her and she was in the bedroom brushing her hair in front of the mirror, getting herself ready for work.

'Take these cheques in for me; give them to Tom when you get there. I'll be in a bit later this morning,' she said, as she handed them to me. Even though she was now eighty-seven, she was still in charge of all the accounts at the shop.

'Course, Grandma. I'm on my way now,' I said, putting the cheques in my pocket. 'See you later.' And I walked back downstairs.

Just as I got to the front door I heard a crash from upstairs. I turned and ran back up and there, lying on the floor, was Grandma, her hairbrush still in her hand.

I bent down shouting. 'Grandma, Grandma, wake up, please.' But she didn't move. She was dead.

I ran to the top of the stairs, calling out for Mum, who was hanging washing in the garden. She ran up the stairs and gasped as she saw her lying there. We managed to lift her onto the bed, and I remember thinking how peaceful she looked. Mum called Uncle and he came down with the rest of the family. I had to leave them, as we had a funeral in the afternoon, and I told Uncle that Jack and I would be able to deal with it, as it was a relatively simple affair.

I was numb. I couldn't believe my lovely grandma had died, and so suddenly – one minute she was there and then the next ... gone!

At services, on a daily basis, I would hear the vicar saying: 'In the midst of life, we are in death', but it was only at that precise moment I fully understood what it meant. I suppose you could say it was a 'wonderful way to go', and for her it was, but to us left behind it was a massive shock. She was a huge part of my life and, together with Uncle Tom, she'd taught me so much about the business. I would miss her so much. The men at the stables were devastated too, as they'd worked with her for over thirty years.

That afternoon, with both of us feeling sad and low, Jack and I finished the funeral at the East London Cemetery. As I came out of the service I was alone and making my way to the car when a voice called me. I turned around and there was Mr Hitchcock, our rival. He was looking at me strangely and it unsettled me, but I didn't know why.

'There's someone to see you, Stan,' he grinned.

'Sorry, Mr Hitchcock, but I don't know what you mean,' I politely answered.

'Round the back there ... go on!' he said, pointing around the corner of the crematorium.

I was puzzled, and shook my head. 'Who is it?' I asked. I didn't know what it was all about, but I certainly wasn't in the mood for jokes, although Mr Hitchcock wasn't famous for his fun personality.

'Bloody hell, boy, go and see ... it's a surprise!'

With that I walked round the back. As I turned the corner there they were – Tommy and Prince. Their heads shot up when they saw me, they whinnied and started to pull the carriage forward, but the coachman stopped them. I couldn't move. I just looked at them. I wanted to run up and hug them but knew I couldn't; then I wanted to run back to the car but knew I couldn't do that either.

As I turned away, Mr Hitchcock was standing silently behind me, sneering. My hands automatically clenched into fists at the sight of him. I started to shake. I wanted to smash his face in, thinking, 'How could you be so cruel?' Then, to make matters even worse, he says, 'Well, don't you want to pat *your* 'orses, Stan?'

I looked straight at him and rage engulfed me. I could feel my hands clenching and un-clenching, but something deep down stopped me. I knew I had to control myself. I couldn't let Uncle down. You know, in some perverse way I think he wanted me to snap, so he could spread the news and try to damage our reputation. So all I said was, 'No thank you, Mr Hitchcock,' and with that I walked past him. As I made my way to the car my legs felt as if they were going to give way, my hands were still clenched, and my eyes were filling with tears. All I could hear behind me was laughter.

As I mentioned earlier, during wartime it never ceased to amaze me how animals and humans adapted to the most horrible of situations, and from that moment it never ceased to astonish me how heartless some people could be.

Years later, Uncle received a phone call from Mrs Hitchcock.

'Mr Cribb,' she said, 'Mr Hitchcock sadly passed away last night and he left strict instructions that I was to call you and ask you if you would conduct his funeral. He said to tell you that he knew you didn't have a lot of time for him, with the rivalry of the two companies and all. He also said to make sure I told you that he had a great admir-ation for you. "Tom Cribb always passed the time of day when our paths crossed," he said, "and I always respected him for that."'

Amazing isn't it, how things turn out.

For all the sadness we had during that horrible year of 1944, the following year proved to be a lot happier. The war was finally over. VE Day or 'Victory in Europe' came on 8 May 1945, virtually a year after the D-Day landings.

Britain was victorious, and everybody was glued to the wireless. The whole nation sat in silence listening to King George VI and Winston Churchill making their speeches. It was an unforgettable moment, especially when Churchill's deep, resounding voice came through:

'This is your victory!' But then the crowd shouted back: 'No, it's yours!' He carried on: *'It is the victory of the cause of freedom in every land. In all our long history we have never seen a greater day than this. Everyone, man or woman, has done their best. Everyone has tried. Neither the long years, nor the dangers, nor the fierce attacks of the enemy, have in any way weakened the unbending resolve of the British nation. God bless you all.'*

There was never in our history a day like this. We were FREE. We had won the war with Germany – six long years of living in constant fear, surrounded by death and destruction was finally over.

They'd been horrible years; petrifying. Relatives, neighbours, friends from school – one day they were with you, the next they were gone. Our childhood had been taken from us; we lived for the day, never knowing what the next would bring ... if you were lucky enough to have a next one. It taught me to cherish every morning, as when the nights drew in and the bombings started you'd never know if you would live to see another.

Street parties were held all over the country but mostly in the East End. It was incredible to witness such jubilation. You could sense a wonderful difference in the atmosphere – relief had replaced terror.

The evil tendrils of the war had reached out and touched every family. I don't believe that one would've been left unscathed. So many of our men, women and children were lost and families would never ever be the same again. As for our magnificent troops, who had fought so hard for their country and for our freedom, one of Churchill's most famous sentences could not have been truer: *'Never in the field of human conflict was so much owed by so many to so few.'*

8

Duration of Emergency
1946 (age 18)

I arrived home from work after one particularly long day and I was shattered, as always. It was normal to see Mum in the scullery preparing our tea when I got home. But something this evening wasn't right. She hadn't called out her usual, 'Hello, Stan, had a good day?' and I couldn't smell any tea cooking on the stove.

As I went into the living room, she was sitting in the armchair, something she never did at that time of the day.

'What's wrong, Mum?' I asked, walking up to her. 'Aren't you well?'

'I'm alright, Stan,' she answered, looking up at me.

'Is it Dad or the girls?' I was starting to get worried.

'No, no they're fine ... this came for you today,' she said, handing over a brown envelope.

I automatically knew what it was, and my heart skipped a beat. On the front was stamped: *On Her Majesty's Service*. I stood there holding it. I wanted to open it but didn't. I just kept looking at it.

'Go on, then, open it, you know what it is,' Mum said.

I tore it open and inside there was a travel permit and a letter that read:

Dear Mr Harris,

You are required to report to The Bedford Barracks on the 16th June 1946 at 12 noon to complete your 'Duration of Emergency' training etc etc.

That was just two weeks away! I was full of emotions, excited, nervous, but also petrified. I'd known it was going to come but now it had I was in a daze.

The 'DOE' or Duration of Service still continued even after the war had finished in 1945. It was to be followed several years later by National Service.

'How do you feel, son?' Mum asked, looking at me with concern. To be honest, I think she was more upset than I was.

'Well, I don't know, I feel strange. I can't take it in... I mean, I've only got two weeks before I have to go. They don't give you much time, do they?' I smiled. I wanted to reassure her that I was OK, as I knew if I didn't she would worry.

'I'm going to miss you so much,' she said, and stood up and hugged me.

'I'm going to miss you too, Mum. But don't worry ... I'll be home on leave, and the time will fly by, you wait and see.'

She then kissed me on the cheek and turned away, heading for the kitchen. 'I'll go and get the tea on,' she said.

Dad was fine about it. I think he was quite excited for me. As the war had finished, the danger aspect had been reduced. There were still dangerous places where I might be deployed but it wouldn't be anything like when the main war was on, or when Dad had served in the 1914–18 World War. He had been just sixteen, (two years under the age for joining up) when he volunteered. He lied about his age, as did so many young men to enable them to fight for their country. He was in the Royal Horse Artillery and he would ride up to the front line next to the big guns, which caused the hearing in his right ear to be permanently damaged. Strangely enough, his horse was called 'Kitty', like my mum, even though it would be another five years before he would meet her.

Kitty was one of the 120,000 horses rounded up in just two weeks from farms and stables up and down the land. These poor horses were removed from their comfortable lives, leaving their owners distraught, and thrown into utter turmoil. Many were forcibly dragged onto ferries at ports all around the country, and if they couldn't be dragged they would be winched on, hanging from huge canvas harnesses. They were then taken to the Western Front and put into battle. These sensitive creatures must have been so bewildered and petrified, as were the soldiers who endured terrible hardships of extreme cold and hunger.

I remember Dad telling me that most of the men didn't have a clue how to look after a horse, so they were given a small booklet from the Blue Cross titled *The Drivers', Gunners' and Mounted Soldiers' Handbook, etc., to Management and Care of Horses and Harness,* which they all kept in their pockets and read religiously. During these bleak, traumatic years, the soldiers and their horses created a unique bond, and this gave the men something to focus on other than the constant threat of death. They would feed, groom and chat to them, and some would even sleep close to their horses for warmth and companionship. Dad told me that when he rode Kitty up to the front line he could feel her trembling with fear between his legs, but she would never back away. The bravery of those men and horses brings tears to my eyes.

Without the 'war horses', Britain could never have won the war, and at the end around 750,000 survived but the majority never received the heroes' welcome they so richly deserved. Around 25,000 of the youngest and fittest were kept but, incredibly, 85,000 were destroyed and their meat used to feed the starving French and the prisoners of war. Around 500,000 were sold to farms in France and Belgium to help restore the countryside and 60,000 made it to Britain where they too were sold. Can you imagine what those years must have been like? I've tried, but I can't even begin to comprehend the fear those boys, men and horses felt. Dad never spoke about the day he was parted from his beloved Kitty, and I think that was because the pain of losing her was too much.

After dinner I got on my bike and went to see Joan. Since her family had moved to Denbigh Road I'd been going round regularly on the pretence of taking bunches of rhubarb from Dad's allotment, as well as the odd bag of potatoes, lettuce and tomatoes, just to see her. I later discovered that all the adults knew we were sweet on one another but they just let me carry on turning up with these food packages because they enjoyed them.

We'd been carrying on like that for a few years. Romances didn't move fast in those days, especially when we were still young and with a war on. But around April 1943, when she reached seventeen, she left me. That's when she decided to join the Women's Land Army. Around 75,000 women joined up over the course of the war to help run small-holdings and to grow fruit and vegetables. She was allocated to Little Hallingbury, Bishops Stortford, Essex, and spent two years with a Mr and Mrs Bass, helping them look after their small farm, which kept cows, turkeys, chickens and rabbits and also provided food for the local community. They loved having her stay with them; she was like the daughter they'd never had.

I missed her so much while she was there, so one Sunday I decided I'd cycle over to visit her. I swear to you, I never did it again. It was around forty miles! I hadn't realised until I was halfway there just how far it was … it was a nightmare. I left at the crack of dawn but when I reached Epping Forest the ground mist suddenly became incredibly thick. It started swirling around my feet, then my legs, and it was soon up to my neck. I literally couldn't see my body. It was so eerie. If anybody had seen me they would've thought it was a ghostly apparition of a bodiless head floating in the early morning mist.

It took me hours to get there and, by the time I arrived, it was almost time to come back. Needless to say I was completely knackered for the rest of the week.

We decided it would be far better for both

of us if she got on a Green Line bus to Epping. I'd meet her there and then we'd travel back together to East Ham on the red bus, then repeat it when she headed back. This worked out a lot better and was far less exhausting!

It was so wonderful when her two years was up and she came back home permanently; it virtually coincided with the war ending, so it was perfect timing. But that happiness was only to last a year as, blow me down, here I am cycling over to tell her I've been called up.

We went to the park and sat on one of the benches, where I showed her the letter. Before she'd even read it she knew what it was. I could see she was upset, but all she said was, 'You'll have a great time, Stan, just like I did in the Land Army. It'll fly by and we can write to one another all the time.'

'But I'm going to miss you so much,' I said, as I put my arm around her.

'I know, and I'm going to miss you too, but we'll see each other every night before you go,' she said, as she laid her head on my shoulder. We sat like that for ages, just talking.

I was dreading telling Uncle Tom the next morning, but would you believe it, all he said was, 'Nothing I can do about it, boy, you've just got to get on with it. God willing we'll still be here when you get back.' That was it – not another word was said.

My last day working was as normal as any other, the only difference being when I left that night, after his usual 'Goodnight, boy, see you in the morning', he left off the 'see you in the morning', adding 'mind how you go, boy'.

He had *very* strange ways – not a man of words or emotions but I knew he'd miss me as much as I would him. Over the last four years I'd settled in to the business and loved getting up for work every day, learning the ropes with him and the other men. I was going to miss them all.

So, on 16 June 1946, I set off to Bedford for my General Military Training, which would last a period of six weeks. Mum and my sisters were in tears when I left, Dad was choked up – which didn't surprise me as he was a big softy – and luckily Joan wasn't there, as I think if she had been I would've burst into tears, too, but I managed to control myself as the neighbours were all out waving me off. It was all a bit embarrassing, to tell you the truth. All that fuss.

I sat on the train, thinking about what was going to happen, where I was going to go, who I was going to meet, and what we would be expected to do – it was overwhelming.

When I got to the barracks, a large group of other young men who'd also just arrived were milling around. It was the first time any of us had been away from home, so we were all filled with trepidation, and in those first few days those feelings were proved right.

We'd all gone from our homes to a boot camp; we knew it was going to be hard but it was certainly a shock to our systems. I'd been mentored by Uncle Tom, who was unbelievably tough, but these sergeant majors ... they were a different species.

I was glad of having had the guidance and support of Mum and Dad and the experience of working with a man like my uncle. This helped me cope with the day-to-day rigours of army life and training. My family had instilled a strong work ethic in me, as well as discipline and taking pride in everything I did which, to be fair, most men had during those times. There weren't any benefits in those days, so no work meant no money; no food and no house. It was as simple as that. So to lie about doing nothing was completely incomprehensible. This mindset certainly made my life in the Army slightly more bearable.

During our training we were taught to clean our rooms, boots and buckles, to make our beds, and to shoot a rifle, as well as take it to bits and clean it. We were paraded, marched and sent on assault courses, all of the time being constantly shouted at morning, noon and night – in fact, when the shouting stopped, you thought you'd gone deaf.

At the end of the six weeks we were allotted a regiment. Three of us were picked out to go into the Royal Armoured Corps 59th Training Regiment, situated in the town of Barnard Castle close to Darlington in County Durham.

Before heading off to our new regiment we were given a week's leave. Seeing Joan, enjoying Mum's cooking, and sleeping in my own bed again was marvellous. She was worried I'd lost weight so she fed me up all week with my favourite meals of steak and kidney pudding, jam roly-poly and spotted dick with Bird's tinned custard. I'm sure London must have run out of suet and custard by the time I left!

So, at the end of this blissful week, I arranged to meet my two friends Bob Gilding and Bobby Hill at King's Cross Station at 3 p.m., where we would catch the train up north. We eventually arrived around 8 p.m. into Darlington station and it was freezing! The gas lamps were lit and flickering on this ghostly cold, dark, miserable station, and it was like we'd reached the bounds of beyond.

Luckily the stationmaster was still around and we asked him how we were supposed to get to Barnard Castle. He pointed across the platform and said, 'Go over there, lads, the train will be along in a while.' It had started to sleet and the wind was howling around the station. As we huddled together on a frozen bench, I longed to be sitting in the armchair next to our fire, eating one of Mum's cakes with a cup of tea, listening to the wireless. But here I was, freezing in this ungodly place.

The three of us sat there, it seemed like ages, waiting for this train, chatting away, once again not knowing what to expect at our new regiment.

We then heard footsteps, *loud* footsteps, coming from a distance. As they got closer we could see they were military; there were three of them, and they were built like bull elephants – a sergeant, a corporal and a lance corporal. They were obviously drill inspectors.

'Don't look at them,' I whispered to the others. 'Let them walk by, we don't want to attract their attention.' As they walked towards us we stood up and saluted.

The sergeant said, 'At ease.' We relaxed and sat down again. The three of them looked so intimidating with their hats pulled down over their eyes and whips tucked under their arms.

We found out later they'd been to the Guards Depot in Pirbright in Surrey and had been on a course which was renowned to 'make or break' new recruits. These three were all here, so they obviously hadn't been broken.

The old steam train eventually arrived. It was only pulling two carriages, so we got in the back whilst the 'whips' got in the front. It took another hour to arrive at Barnard Castle. Well, I thought Darlington station was bad enough, but this! It was as if we'd reached the 'end of the line' – in fact, I'm sure it was. There was virtually nothing there, just a small hut, which was the station, surrounded by fields. It was dark and bitterly cold, the wind was still howling and we had no idea where we should be heading. There was nobody around to ask and no signposts. Just then the doors of the front carriages opened and we watched the three 'whips' climb off and walk up a path that ran alongside the station. They opened a gate, climbed a few steps and carried on up the hill. They clearly knew where they were going so we followed behind at a respectable distance.

We'd walked a mile or so through driving sleet, uphill, against the bitterly cold wind, overcoats pulled tightly round us and hats pulled down as far as they'd go to stop our ears from dropping off. We were in the dark but fortunately we had our torches to guide us and of course the 'whips' up ahead kept us on track. God only knows how we were supposed to have found the place if it hadn't been for them. What a relief when we saw the barracks in the distance – however, the cold we felt that night would be nothing to that in the coming weeks; the winter of 1946 turned out to be one of the coldest on record.

On the first morning we were told to attend the exercise halls in a singlet, socks, shorts and boots. Now, that was OK if we were going to stay inside, but no, that would be far too civilised. As I discovered they didn't do 'civilised' in the Army.

Lance Corporal Brown, who happened to be one of the 'whips', marches in, champing at the bit to practise his newly discovered skills on us poor buggers.

He bellowed, 'Right, outside you lot... NOW!'

We all ran outside and, within seconds, our teeth were chattering and we were literally turning blue.

'I want you to RUN down to the town and back again without stopping. Notice I say RUN, not stroll, walk or jog, and I certainly don't want to hear about any gassing with the local girls. Just keep going till you're back here. WELL, GO ON, what are you bleedin' waiting for – for me to kiss you goodbye. GO!'

And off we went. It was freezing cold and icy underfoot, so how we didn't break our necks or get pneumonia, God only knows.

Needless to say, he didn't come with us; he had a spy waiting at the halfway point down in the village, ticking our names off a list and making sure we didn't turn back. They were hard bastards.

Due to the atrocious weather, we were regularly sent out on patrols to help save sheep stranded on the hills. Sheep are renowned for being the most stupid animals on the planet and, believe me, they are! As snow starts to fall, instead of heading back to their farms they just carry on eating and, before they know it, they're snowed in and it's left to us to dig the dopey beggars out. So off we went, heading to the field where the farmer had told us the sheep were stuck. We then dug out a trench in order for the sheep to run back along. The snow by then could be 3-4 feet deep and digging it out was backbreaking – the only bonus being you got warm doing it.

If we hadn't found them by lunchtime we would then dig an igloo; in fact we quite liked these, as they were really cosy once they'd been made. We used to climb into them and someone from the Catering Corps would bring up our lunch, which normally consisted of meat and veg and we would sit in the igloo eating and talking, drinking mugs of tea. Unfortunately these pleasant brief interludes didn't last long, as we then had to carry on sheep hunting. I couldn't wait to get out of that place and be posted on proper manoeuvres

We ended up spending eight torturous weeks there. I'm trying to think of a useful word to describe it: 'bleak' just doesn't do it justice. Perhaps desolate, dismal, god-forsaken, wretched, would suit better, or maybe one I haven't thought of. In fact, I always remember thinking during my time in Barnard Castle Barracks that God must have had a right cob on when he created that place.

At last our orders came through – we were to join the King's Royal 15/19th Hussars and we were then sent on manoeuvres. Over the next eighteen months we had tours of duty in Egypt, Palestine, Jordan and Khartoum.

Looking back, I must admit I enjoyed most of my time during my 'DOE'. It was an experience I've certainly never regretted or forgotten. The only part of it I could've done without was when I contracted malaria in Jordan and was delirious for weeks in a hospital in Jaffa. Thankfully I got over it and I've never had a relapse, although I'm sure that if years later you'd mentioned it to Uncle, he would've said that most of the time I seemed delirious.

The type of camaraderie you get in the services, especially when you're in dangerous environments (in which we found ourselves during tours in Palestine, with the 'Stern' gang who were 'Fighters for the Freedom of Israel', and the Irgun Zvai Leumi, who were a militant terrorist organisation), is hard to find and, when you do, it's something to be relished. I met some marvellous men and made some great friends – one being Bob Gilding from Poplar, whom I mentioned before.

I got a call a few years back from his wife, who told me Bob had sadly died and that he always told her he wanted me to conduct his funeral. When I went round to sort everything out, she said he'd left something for me upstairs on the cabinet next to his bed. I went up and there was a small box waiting. I opened it and inside was his regimental scarf and cufflinks, which I still have to this day.

After being away for so long it was good to be home. Although food was still scarce, Mum had managed to rustle up a delicious tea for my homecoming and we all sat around to enjoy it. Everyone wanted to hear my stories, even the neighbours, who kept popping in and out during the evening to welcome me home.

My sisters and Mum were outside washing up and I was sitting down talking with Dad. He looked quite serious as he leant forward in his armchair. 'It's great to have you back, Stan. We've certainly all missed you and I can't believe how much you've grown. It's as if twenty-two months ago you went away a boy and sitting in front of me now is a fine young man. Me and your mum are very proud of you.'

'Stop it, Dad, I'm getting all embarrassed,' I said, laughing. 'But it is *great* to be home.'

He leant back into the chair. 'So, now you're back what do you intend to do?' he asked, looking at me intently.

I looked at him puzzled. 'Do ... what d'you mean?'

'With your work, son. What d'you mean to do in regards to work?' His voice had become a bit agitated and his fingers were tapping on the arms of the chair.

It seemed like a trick question ... now I *was* confused! Dad wouldn't do trick questions so I replied, 'Ummm ... well, what I did before I left: go back with Uncle Tom.'

'Dear God, no!' he sighed, shaking his head. 'I always thought that was a passing phase. I hoped by the time you got home from service you would've got it out of your system once and for all. You don't seem to realise the importance of a job with a pension. That's one of the reasons I joined the police. You know if you go back to work with Uncle Tom you'll never be guaranteed a pension. How would you survive when you retire?'

'But you *know* I've never thought about doing anything else. I don't care about a pension. I'm only twenty. I'm not thinking of when I retire!'I was shocked. I hadn't been expecting this.

I noticed it had gone all quiet in the kitchen.

'I know and *that's* the problem; you're not thinking ahead, you're just living for today, which is wrong ... you should be planning ahead. Believe me, son, you're young today but trust me when I tell you, and it'll happen quicker than you think, you'll turn around and you'll be in your fifties and it'll seem like only yesterday we were sitting having this conversation ... then where will you be?'

'I'll just have to deal with that when it comes, Dad.'

'So, what you're saying is that there's *nothing* else that you'd want to do except be an undertaker – is that right?' he asked.

'That's right, *nothing!*' I was now getting angry. I thought everything was fine before I'd left; we'd already gone through this years before.

What on earth had brought this on?

With that, he let out a deep sigh. He pushed himself out of the chair, as if it was an effort to get up. He then walked over to the sideboard, opened a drawer and took out a box. He started going through a pile of papers and, near to the bottom, he pulled

144

out a blue form. He opened it, glanced at it and then started to tear it up.

'What are you doing, Dad?' I was now completely confused. 'What's that you're tearing up?

'You've made your mind up to be an undertaker and I have to accept that's what you want to do with your life. I always hoped you'd change your mind along the way ... I've had this form since you were two years old, you know.' He looked sad.

'Two!'I said, stunned. 'What on earth is it?'

'It's an application form for the police,' he said, looking over at me. I saw he was upset. I didn't know what to say, I just sat there looking at him. But then the penny dropped. All those years ago when Uncle Tom had come to the school to see if I wanted to join the business, my excitement that evening while we were having tea – and Dad trying to persuade me to go into another profession with a pension – this is what it was all about. *Now* I understood the 'look' that went between him and Mum – it all made sense. He had been waiting all this time, hoping I would join him in the police force and follow on the family tradition as he and his father had done.

I sat there feeling guilty. 'I don't know what to say, Dad, I never knew...'

'It's alright, son. I think deep down I've

known for a very long time that it wouldn't be needed.'

From that day on, not another word was mentioned about our conversation.

When I returned to work the following morning, there was Uncle, where I'd left him twenty-two months beforehand, behind his desk in the shop.

'Hello, Uncle, I'm back!' I said cheerily.

'Welcome home, boy,' he smiled. That's all he said. Good job I wasn't the sensitive type.

That night I went to see Joan; I couldn't wait to see her. We'd written hundreds of letters to each other while I was away, and we were now desperate to be together. So, not long after being home, I plucked up the courage to propose.

I did it properly. I got dressed up in my best suit (I left off my top hat) and went to ask Mr Davies for his daughter's hand. Thank goodness he was delighted but, call me an old cynic, thinking back on it he was probably considering all the extra fruit and veg he'd be getting from our allotment!

We had a small tea to celebrate, which was only for our immediate families. Rationing was still in force, and getting any extra food for parties or celebrations was difficult. Sometimes relatives or friends would give you their coupons in order for you to get something special, but fancy items could be found on the black market if you had a grocer who was 'in the know' which, to be honest, most of them were.

So there we were, having all had a lovely, enjoyable evening. We were so excited about our engagement and forthcoming marriage. As we sat around the conversation turned, as it normally did in those days, back to the war years. There was a lull when all of a sudden Joan's dad bangs his fist down hard on the table, making us all jump.

'Goodness, Frank, what on earth's the matter?' Joan's mum said, turning to him.

'I'm sorry,' he said. 'But just thinking about it makes my blood boil!'

'What's that?' my dad asked.

'Just living through those war years was bad enough, wasn't it? Never knowing from one day to the next if you'd survive, then you get bombed out of your own home that you've spent time and hard-earned money making as nice as you can, and then something like that happens!'

Boy, is he angry!

'What on earth happened, Frank?' Mum asked sympathetically.

'I know it's seven or eight years ago, but some things you just don't forget, do you. After we were bombed out some dirty rotten bastard – excuse my French, ladies – only got into our house and nicked my toilet door, didn't he? Absolute disgrace, nicking somebody's toilet door. I mean, how low can you get?'

He was glaring at me, not for any particular reason, thank heavens, just because he was angry, but Dad's head swings around and now he's looking at me too!

Joan looks at him. 'Oh, Dad, you're not *still* going on about that!' She then turned to us. 'You wouldn't believe it, if we've heard about his precious toilet door once we've heard it a thousand times.'

'Well, what d'you expect! I still can't believe someone could do such a thing!'He then turns to me. 'What do you think, Stan, do you think I'm overreacting?'

I swallow. 'No, not at all. I mean it's, it's ... terrible! How could somebody do something like that?'

'I don't know, son, I really don't know,' he said, leaning back in his chair, shaking his head. 'People never cease to amaze me, they really don't.You'll appreciate that as you get older.'

The evening fortunately ended shortly afterwards. When they'd gone, Dad looked at me and grinned.

'WHAT?' I said, trying to look serious.

'What indeed!You crafty little sod ... after all this time ... but it did come in bloody handy, didn't it?'

9

Mrs O'Leary and Miss Holmes
1949 (age 21)

As walked into the shop one day, Uncle was sitting at the desk, coming to the end of a phone conversation.

Since I'd been home from my military service he had reinstated me at the shop in Rathbone. He wanted to train me up to organise and conduct funerals, and when business was slack he would be able to teach me how to French polish the coffins. He was a master at that – in fact, he was a master at all things funereal – but, outside of that, his character left a lot to be desired. I could see why he'd never got married; he could be so difficult he would've proved an impossible spouse. He seemed contented on his own, though; never a man for going down the pub or socialising, his true love was pottering around in his beloved garden, and he'd always try to secure tickets for any boxing nights going on in the area.

He'd taught me coffin-making down at the yard. That skill (then it *was* a skill – nowadays they wouldn't know what hit them if they had to make one from scratch) took me around a year to perfect.

Remember, we used raw timber then. When it arrived at the workshop the tree was sliced into planks but the bark was still intact. As I mentioned before, we only used elm and oak, as these have a lovely grain and show up to perfection once polished. The thickness of the wood was over 1" (we also supplied a 'Cribb special', which was one and a half inches) so this, along with the solid brass handles, made it an extremely heavy object – and that was before the body was in it. I sometimes wonder how on earth we lifted them, as they weighed a ton. I recall coming home one evening after a particularly busy day and when I took off my jacket my shirt covering my right shoulder was smothered in blood and red raw from carrying the coffins. In fact, to this day, that shoulder is quite a lot lower than my left.

In most situations, Uncle would be extremely impatient; he couldn't abide people dithering but once he got into the workshop he was in his element. He would spend hours showing me how to plane down the coffins, to shape and fit them together, and he loved the tricky bit of creating the 'kerfs' at the top end. These shaped the area where the shoulders would fit, and that, without doubt, was the hardest section to make. After that the coffin was lined in a thick calico and then the satin insert and ruffles would be fitted. The lining was a necessity in the days before embalming as it would absorb some of the body's fluids and prevent them leaking through the joints.

One day I was in the workshop, halfway through making a coffin, when he walked in to check on everyone. I was hammering a nail when I heard a bellow from across the workshop: 'You're a coffin-maker, boy, not a sodding watchmaker. Put some welly into it, for Christ's sake!'

So I too had, at last, now mastered the art of coffin-making and I was onto the next process of staining and polishing. That was a skill in its own right as well. It would take around four hours of continual work to get a coffin perfected. And all of this process was carried out in the shop window, so passers-by could stand and watch. At first I was really self-conscious about having an audience but, once I'd got over my initial shyness, I must admit I actually enjoyed it.

In fact, standing in that shop window was an education in itself. It opened my eyes to a lot of things, especially during the war years when everything was in short supply. But before I explain to you about the art of polishing, let me tell you about Jimmy the Grocer.

You've heard of the Alfred Hitchcock film *Rear Window* – well, this was our version:

Front Window.

Directly across from us was a grocer's shop, selling the bits and pieces allocated to us through rationing books: butter, sugar, flour, tea, that sort of thing. The proprietor was the type of grocer I mentioned earlier – someone you went to when you wanted something 'extra special'.

These are the men who would normally find themselves in trouble with the police, as they would be offered all sorts of goodies sold 'under the counter' – the likes of tinned salmon, corned beef and the odd hock of ham. More often than not, these items had come from the docks.

Most dockers were honest men but, like in any large business, there were a few who strayed from the tracks. Generally they were the main suppliers of these goodies, as they had access to the ships that brought them in, so on occasions when the odd box of food was going begging, it proved too tempting for them to walk away. They saw an opportunity and took it. I couldn't blame them; many of these men had over a dozen children, and to get a few extra bob in their pockets at the end of the week meant being able to feed and clothe them, so nobody begrudged them a few perks here and there. They were tough old days, and if you saw a way to put some extra food on the table you grabbed it.

The grocer's was originally owned by Bill

(or, as he was more commonly known, 'Bacon Bill'). He retired through ill health so, after the war, his brother Jimmy left the RAF and returned to take over the business. Like Bill, he was a lovely man – both of them were very kind and would always try to help anybody out.

Jimmy'd always flirt with the female customers, and they all loved it. He wasn't a film star or anything; he was tall and rotund with a huge handlebar moustache, which he used to curl up at the ends. In the summer months, when it was hot, we used to prop our front door open to let the breeze in and you could always hear him chatting to his customers in his big booming voice.

Shortly after you saw a woman walk into his shop you'd hear things like: 'Goodness me, it's Peggy Peck! Just for a second there I thought Lana Turner had walked in ... my mistake ... what can I do for you today, Peggy?' Or 'Good afternoon, Dolly! Did I ever tell you my favourite auntie was called Dolly? It's a name that holds a great affection for me and may I also add that your hair looks particular fetching today; you've done something different to it, haven't you? I noticed Ingrid Bergman had a very similar style when I saw her at the cinema last night. May I say that Mr Dolly is a *very* lucky man!' And so on.

That's all we heard coming from his shop.

He certainly cheered up our day; every woman that went in there was likened to one film star or another, and to see them leave ... they'd come out, one by one, flushed and giggling to themselves, looking around conspiratorially as if they'd had some secret assignation. So he not only brightened our day, he brightened theirs too. In fact, every person who walked through his door would come out better off in one way or another.

His heart was as big as his belly. Any child you saw going into his shop with or without its mother would come out biting into a chunk of Spam. No child went hungry around him.

The problem all grocers had with 'under the counter' trading was the penalties. Due to rationing the police were under strict instructions to arrest anyone found engaged in these types of dealings, and a *huge* fine and generally imprisonment was normal. It was a very risky business to get involved in.

With these shenanigans, if you're not caught it encourages you to carry on, but with bigger and bigger contraband, and that, sadly, is exactly what happened to Jimmy.

We tried to keep an eye out for him, but it would only be a matter of time before he was caught. In our front window we had stone statues on show that would be pur-chased to decorate graves: Our Lady, St Patrick and Our Lord etc. Behind these was a wooden panel that separated the window display from the inside of the shop. On the left-hand wall as you entered was a large cabinet with two glass doors, which if positioned at the correct angles, enabled me to see way down Rathbone Street, virtually to the junction of the Barking Road, and I could spot any policeman on patrol coming our way. They'd all tended to make a beeline for our shop, as they'd become regular visitors to our back office, where they'd sit drinking coffee and having a smoke. When I saw them coming, I'd pop out the back, put a saucepan on the stove with a spoonful of coffee grains in it ready for when they arrived.

Nobody in the area wanted to see Jimmy go to prison so, if I saw a policeman down the road, I'd just pop over and tip him the wink. If I didn't do it somebody else would. In fact, when you saw the police approaching you'd always hear some type of signal – a particular whistle or a car hooter blasting out to let everyone know the police were on their way. I loved the fact that everyone looked out for each other.

The police would come into the shop normally one at a time, but occasionally they'd all meet up for their coffee break. It was OK, I didn't mind, but it did stop me from working, which could be a nuisance sometimes, as I couldn't tell them to 'sod off'.

One particular day the phone rang and a frustrated voice on the line said, 'Sergeant James, Plaistow Station. You got any of my men there?'

'Er, no, not seen any today, sergeant,' I lied.

'Look, I'm not gonna have a go, but if any of them are there, tell them to get their arses back, 'cos I'm running an empty station here and the inspector's due any minute.' And with that he hung up.

I turned to the men. 'Your sergeant's looking for you ... apparently the inspector's on his way. You'd better get going, 'cos he doesn't sound very happy.'

Hearing that, they turned into the 'Keystone Kops', hands fumbling trying to get their boots back on, jacket buttons being done up wrong, helmets dropped – it was chaos. Two ran out the back way, grabbing their bikes as they went, the other through the front, all of them scattering in different directions.

After a few minutes, the whistles and car hooters were heard again, this time slightly differently. Obviously it was the lookouts' interpretation of the 'all clear'.

One day, I was standing looking out the front, when I noticed a 'mechanical horse' coming slowly up the road. These were three-wheeled tractor-type vehicles with canvas canopies over the back trailer.

They were used a lot on the railways at the time. They'd been around since 1934 and had been invented because the railway companies were looking for a suitable vehicle to replace the horse-drawn carriages that delivered parcels to towns.

It pulled up and the driver got out. He started strolling towards Jimmy's. He stopped along the way, lighting a cigarette and casually looking around; he then carried on walking before disappearing into the shop. A few minutes later he's heading back to the 'horse'. He pulls away, driving past our shop and turns into the side road, where Jimmy's storerooms are located. I'm now smiling to myself; I know something's going to happen but don't know what.

The driver approaches the side door and a chap's standing there holding a wooden plank. The mechanical horse stops, the plank is pushed onto the edge of it, with the other end on the pavement, the canopy flies up, and three *enormous* round cheeses come rolling down, shooting straight into the side of the building. It was like watching the scene with the bouncing bombs from the film *The Dambusters*. It all happened so quickly that if you'd blinked you would've missed it. The driver whips the 'horse' around 360 degrees, turns back onto the main road, parks a few hundred yards up, gets out and walks back to pick up his 'cut'.

I waited an hour or so, then popped over to get a nice chunk of cheese for my tea; now *that's* what I'd call the perks of the job!

But unfortunately Jimmy didn't stop with cheeses. He got involved in a far more dangerous enterprise. Early one morning I saw three brand-new Austin cars being parked along the side road outside his storeroom.

Just then, Uncle walks in. 'What you grinning at?' he said, turning back to look out the window.

'Don't know yet, but they're up to something over the road and I'm waiting to see what happens,' I explained. We both then turned back to watch.

These cars had come from the Austin factory in Birmingham. They were literally just off the production line and were being driven to the docks to be transported to Europe. But before they reached their final destination they were being taken on a detour past Jimmy's, and it definitely wasn't for him to view the fine workmanship.

Suddenly there was a frenzy of activity. It was like watching a pit-stop at a Grand Prix. One end of a hose was pushed into the car's tank, whilst the other end went into a chap's mouth. He then proceeded to suck it up; as the petrol reached his mouth he pulled it out and held it over a large tin can, siphoning it out until the tank was virtually empty. As this was going on, another bloke was swiping the spare tyre out of the back and another, having started the engine, was now removing the battery. Apparently if you start a car and then remove its battery it will keep running until you turn off the ignition (I told you the view was an education). Three cars were done in about ten minutes and all the time a lookout was on each corner.

'Can you believe it?'I said, grinning, turning to Uncle. 'He's pushing his luck this time.'

He just stood there shaking his head. 'I tell you, boy, this'll all end in tears, you mark my words,' he said, heading back into the office.

'Miserable old bugger,' I thought. But unfortunately he would be proved right.

Once the cars had been stripped of spare tyres and pilfered of petrol, the drivers who'd brought them down from the factory jumped back in and drove them up the road. They turned into Hallsville Road, onto the brow of the bill at Silvertown Way and, in neutral gear, coasted them down to the docks to save the last remnants of petrol left in the tanks. God only knows what happened when they got to the docks. The delivery men obviously parked in their allocated area and left the keys with the security staff, but how they got the cars onto the ships once that engine had been turned off I've no idea. I assume they were pushed on and it was left to the dockers at the other end to deal with the problem.

However it was done, this practice went on fortnightly over a number of months and then it stopped – obviously they were being rattled and the Law were closing in.

But the funny thing was, every Wednesday night, without fail, when the policemen got their pay packets you'd always see a row of bikes lined up alongside Jimmy's wall. They were all in there getting their share of the goodies!

Sadly for everyone in the area, a new group of policemen arrived on the beat, and one of them obviously wanted to make a name for himself. Within a month of him arriving Jimmy was arrested for black-market dealings and was imprisoned. It was a terrible day, seeing the Black Maria draw up and a group of police go in and take him. As I said, for all of his dodgy dealings, he gave away so much to the poor in the area; they knew if they went to see him, he'd always put that extra pat of butter or another couple of eggs into their sparse shopping baskets.

It's always the same, isn't it? You'll always get one bugger who wants to ruin it for everybody else.

He received a two-year sentence. Unfortunately, for whatever reason, on his release he never returned to our neck of the woods.

Right, now you've heard the story of the

goings-on from our front window, I can get back to the intricacies of French polishing. Although, thinking about it now, I don't know how I ever got round to it with all the other entertainment going on around me.

Firstly you would put on your apron. Now aprons were *very* important – obviously they protected your clothes but also you were on show; you were in the front window for the 'world and his wife' to come and watch you, so you had to be immaculate, even though you were polishing. My apron would be taken home and washed every night; there was never a mark or blemish on it and, if there was, another would be used. It would be pressed and starched and even the apron ties would be starched too.

You could always tell the quality of a coffin-maker when interviewing him by his toolbox. All had a personal toolbox and the way it was presented – and obviously the condition of his apron – spoke volumes about the man's character and work ethic.

To start, linseed oil and plaster of Paris were mixed into a paste; this would then be smoothed onto the sides to fill in any gaps between the joints, and the residue scraped off. Once that was dry it could be sandpapered down, so it was completely smooth. After that, the stain would be applied and then the elbow grease came to the front with the polishing. We would make a 'dolly', which was made of calico and stuffed with wadding; this was dabbed into a polish pot and rubbed in small circles over the entire area. The finish, when it was done properly, of course, was something to be proud of. To think you had literally made the whole coffin from scratch gave you a feeling of great achievement.

One particular morning I was just getting my apron on to start polishing when Uncle hangs up the phone. 'Put that apron back on, boy, that was a call from Miss Holmes. Her sister died last night, unexpectedly. She wants me to go and collect the body from the hospital, then I'll have to go round and see her to make the arrangements. So I'm going to have to leave it to you to take Mr O'Leary back home. I'll see you back here later.'

I'd become a bit braver as I'd got older, so I said, 'Couldn't I go to collect Miss Holmes and you take Mr O'Leary home?'

'Why's that?' he says, looking at me funny.

'Well, I know this sounds daft, but I don't think Mrs O'Leary likes me very much.' I sounded pathetic but it was true. She was terrifying; the type of woman you wouldn't want to meet down a dark alley after she'd had a few milk stouts. You could imagine her bashing the living daylights out of you if you just looked at her the wrong way. No, she wasn't for me. (In fact, I don't know who she would've been for, but her and Mr O'Leary had been married for around forty years, so he obviously loved her.)

'You don't think she likes you... Bloody hell, I've heard it all now! What is it – a popularity contest? You daft sod, you're conducting her husband's funeral, not wanting her to adopt you! Get your suit on and get down there NOW!' Shaking his head, he stood up, then picked up his bowler hat and patted it down on his head. 'Right, I'm off! See you later. Send my regards to Mrs O'Leary, and tell her not to speak too harshly to you as it upsets you ... and tell her I'll be there in ten days to take them to the cemetery.'

I don't know why I bothered. I should've learnt by now that I wouldn't get any sympathy from him, or any other member of my family for that matter.

I went round to the workshop and collected Mr O'Leary. In the East End, the 'Chapel of Rest' wouldn't be introduced until the 1960s. Everyone was 'laid out' in their front rooms in those days. They'd be left there for between seven to ten days. Can you imagine, during the warmer months, what effect this would have on the body?

We put his coffin in the hearse, with a crucifix and five large candle-holders, and headed around to his house in Katherine Road. As I walked up to the front door I saw that the 'black board' was still nailed onto the front window frame. Many mourners requested this when they came to the shop to make arrangements on the day the person had died. Within a few hours of them leaving I would be around to their house, fixing the board to the window, where it would stay until the funeral was conducted. It would signify to the neighbourhood that there had been a death in the house.

I knocked on the door, which was quickly opened by Mrs O'Leary, dressed as always completely in black, her long, full skirt down to her ankles and her steel-grey hair pulled back tightly in a bun. She was only around 5ft tall but she had such an imposing air. Around her neck was a large wooden crucifix, resting against her enormous chest. The O'Learys were one of the staunchest Catholic families I've come across, and Mrs O'Leary was the godmother of it ... or she was to me, anyway.

Trying to peer around me, she says sharply, in her broad Irish brogue, 'And where's *Mr Cribb?*'

I stood up as tall as I could, trying to reach my maximum height, which was now around 6' 1". I hoped it might help me, psychologically – it didn't!

'He sends his sincere apologies, Mrs O'Leary. He was called away to an urgent job this morning. He said to tell you that he'll *certainly* be here to conduct the funeral of your husband.' I cleared my throat. *So far so good!*

Then, bugger me, her eyes went all slitty. 'Did ya bring the candlesticks and crucifix?' she quizzed me. I knew she was hoping I'd say I'd forgotten them so she could kick-off.

'I certainly have, Mrs O'Leary, they're all in the hearse.'

'How many did ya bring, boy?' she asked.

'Five, as you requested,' I replied confidently.

'Oh!' She was clearly disappointed. 'You'd better bring 'im in, then. Ya know where ya have to take him. Call me when you're done.'

And with that she walks off down the hall, her hips so broad you could hear the swishing of her skirt as it brushed against the walls.

I carried the candles and crucifix into the front room. It was arranged in the style of how many Catholic families liked to prepare their 'laying out' rooms. Everything that could reflect the body or the coffin had been covered in white sheets, as it was believed that the deceased's spirit could be trapped in the reflection of mirrors and glass cabinets. All clocks in the house were stopped at the time of death. Some people even turned the photos of family and friends down to prevent any of them being possessed by the exiting spirit.

I placed the candlesticks in a circle with the

crucifix in the middle on a table that had already been set out for me, and lit the candles. The Irish Catholics in olden times would burn twelve reed canes in place of candles, to scare the devils from the departing soul, but in modern times five candles were used in place of the canes to create a 'circle of five', which was supposed to be protection from the powers of darkness.

On a small table a bowl of snuff, tobacco and several clay pipes had been left ready for the start of the wake – which was offered to the friends and relatives who would be attending. It was expected of them to take at least a ceremonial puff or two when it was offered, even if they didn't smoke, as it was classified as an insult if you didn't. Food and drink would be added as guests arrived.

We then carried the coffin in, lying it across four chairs that had been placed close to the open window. This would be left open for several hours, to allow the spirit to depart the body, then it was closed. I removed the lid and propped it in the corner of the room. In some Irish funerals the body would be removed and placed onto a table and the coffin would then be left propped up in the corner. It was removed in order for the 'watchers' to have a clear, unobstructed view to see if they witnessed any signs of life.

Everything was prepared, so I went along and told 'the godmother' we'd finished and would be on our way.

'Oh no, don't t'ink you'll be going anywhere just yet!' she said, looking up at me, her eyes going slitty again. I wished she wouldn't do that, it gave me the creeps; she reminded me of a snake preparing to strike its prey. 'I want to see everyt'ink's done properly.' So she starts marching – I don't think she *walked* anywhere – up the passage to the front room. As she marched in, she let out a little gasp, stopping dead in her tracks. It was the first time I'd seen or heard any emotion from her. She walked slowly up to the coffin and looked down at her husband's face.

This was always a difficult time for us, the moment the bereaved saw their loved ones for the first time since they died. It was more than likely they'd only died the day before, and more times than not, in that house, so it was distressing for the person to see them just twenty-four hours later, in a coffin.

She bent down over him, closely inspecting his face. It looked like she was going to kiss him. But she didn't – she stood straight back up and waved a stubby finger at him, shouting, 'I said ya'd drink yerself to frigging death. You're a frigging eejit, so you are!'

I didn't know what I should do; she hadn't told me I could leave, so I just stood there. She held onto the side of the coffin and knelt down. When she eventually managed to get down I bent my head and closed my eyes, thinking I should say a prayer with her, when I heard her booming voice.

'What the bleedin 'ell ya doing, boy? What would ya be having ya eyes shut at a time like this for? Will ya pass me the frigging candlestick? Me knees won't be holdin' out much longer!' With that, I grabbed the stick and handed it to her, now completely confused. God help me, where was Uncle Tom when I needed him?

Bending under the coffin, she started running the candle along the bottom. At last she leant back and handed me the stick. But she couldn't get back up, so she gripped onto the side of the coffin, trying to pull herself up.

'Christ!' I thought. 'It's going to tip up and Mr O'Leary's going to land right on top of her!'

I quickly moved forward. 'Please be careful, let me help you,' I said, starting to worry and, with that, I stood behind her and lifted her up with my arms under her armpits. I'm not joking – she was actually heavier than one of our 'Cribb specials'. As we stood there, both puffing, she turned to me.

'I suppose you'll be wondering why I'm looking under the coffin, boy? You hear a lot about undertakers putting all sorts of things on the bottom of coffins. They leave the proper wood for where you can see it. I've been in your workshop years ago when your grandfather was there, and I've seen 'im put a patch in a piece of wood better than I could in the arse of me ol' man's trousers, and that'll be the trut'!'

I cleared my throat. 'I think you will find, Mrs O'Leary, that at Cribb and Son we do not participate in those sorts of practices. Was everything to your satisfaction?'

She sniffed. 'It was, boy.' She was definitely cheesed off; I think she'd been looking forward to exposing an old patched-up door at the bottom.

'Now, I've got to get everyt'ing prepared for the wake, so you be off,' she said, shooing me out with her hand.

I made my way back to the shop feeling quite jubilant. I'd faced my demons – or should I say demon – face to face and not cracked under the pressure.

The history of the wake had always fascinated me. It was initially known as 'watching' and became a recognised institution. It was originally an old Jewish custom. The body would be placed in a sepulchre, unsealed for three days, during which time the body was visited by relations, hoping to see signs of life.

In Christian practice, a gathering of friends and relatives would, in the presence of the body, offer special prayers for the deceased when it was thought that the soul would be passing into another state.

There is also evidence of professional 'watchers' – not only in the past but today too. They'd be paid to 'watch' the body from the time of death to the time of the funeral. The poor were normally obliged to shorten the period between death and burial, so they could reduce the charges. The social status of the bereaved families was estimated by the length of time they were able to hold out to the exorbitant demands of the watcher, but it was considered an honour to employ their services.

This ritual began many centuries ago, when lead cups were used to drink ale or whisky, and the combination would occasionally knock the recipients out for days. Everybody who saw them just presumed they were dead, but in fact they were in a coma. They would be laid out on the kitchen table whilst family and friends would gather around, eat and drink and wait to see if the person would wake up. This process started when it was discovered that people had been buried alive.

In the Victorian era, coffins would be dug up in order for the old graves to be reused, as there wasn't available space to keep digging new ones. In fact, the diary of a gentleman from 1859 reveals: *'It is said that at the present time in London it is more difficult to find room for the dead than it is for the living.'* Once

the coffins were opened they were destroyed
and the bones taken off to a 'bone house' –
buildings where human skeletal remains
would be stored. It was when these coffins
were opened that the grim discovery was
made. Unbelievably one in twenty-five was
found to have scratch marks on the inside.

When people heard about this they were
obviously petrified it would happen to them
or their loved ones, so they decided to take
matters into their own hands to avoid it happening again. So an ingenious device was
put into practice. A string would be tied
around the wrist of the corpse, which was
then fed through a small hole in the top of
the coffin and attached to a bell on top of the
grave. So if they 'came to' and found themselves entombed, they'd tug the string to ring
the bell. Someone would then sit in the
graveyard morning and night for several
days, listening for the bell to ring so they
could be quickly dug out and saved from the
horrors of being buried alive. That's where
the sayings 'saved by the bell' and 'the graveyard shift' originate. Although in reality they
would never have survived days, as their
oxygen would have run out after around two
hours.

Uncle Tom arrived back with a huge grin on
his face, having been to arrange Miss
Holmes's funeral. If I'd had my Box Brownie

camera to hand, I would've taken a photo, as it was such a rare occurrence.

'Well, you certainly look like you've had a good time,' I said.

'I tell you what, boy, not many things shock me and make me laugh at the same time, as I'm sure you've noticed, especially in this business, but Miss Holmes did both today.' He paused for a second to light up a Woodbine. Taking a deep draw he said, 'I'm parched; make me a cuppa first, then I'll tell you what happened.'

I did as he requested; I was certainly looking forward to hearing his story. I had witnessed more eclipses than seen him in this good a mood.

I put the tea down next to him. 'So, what happened?' I asked, eagerly sitting down opposite.

'Well, we'd been sitting there discussing the funeral. She'd decided on the elm casket for her sister ... you knew her sister Eleanor, didn't you?'

'No, not really,' I answered.

'No, thinking about it, I don't suppose you did. Bit before your time. Well, they've always lived in Macaulay Road for as long as I can remember. They moved there an age ago, from Scotland – must have been around the 1900s. Neither of them married, and as far as anyone was aware they never had any "gentleman callers", if you know what I mean. I often saw them walking about, very attractive women they were, always smartly dressed. I always remember Mum talking about them one day to a neighbour, discussing what a mystery they were. You know how women love a gossip ... never happy unless they're pulling some poor bugger to bits. Anyway, once she's decided on the casket and handles I start to explain about the ruffles. She asks what the ruffles are, so I explain it's the name for the satin inserts that line the inside of the casket, and there are also ruffles around the edge. I told her there was a variety of colours to choose from, and she was surprised at this. So I went into more detail, you know, explaining what the colours were for. My exact words were, "If you were asking me, Miss Holmes, which colour I would choose for your sister, I would suggest white."

"'White?'" she says, in that soft, cultured Scottish accent of hers, sipping her tea. "That's interesting, and why may I ask would you choose white, Mr Cribb?"

"'Well,'" I say. "Your sister was a maiden lady and white signifies purity, so in my mind it would seem the appropriate choice."

"'Oh, I see,'" she says. "*Now* I understand what you are saying! So what other colours do you have, and who would they be used for? I wasn't aware that the colours signified the character of the person inside."

'So I then sit forward and start to explain.

'"Oh, indeed, Miss Holmes," I say. "To me, it's an important factor and must be correct for the individual concerned. Let me explain: lemon is very popular for younger people, teenagers normally; obviously we have pale blue and pink for very young children and purple of course for the older, more – well, I'm not sure of the word I would use – maybe 'worldly' would be suitable."

'"Yes, yes, I see. I know *exactly* what you mean, Mr Cribb. Thank you so much for explaining everything to me. I hadn't realised," she says.

'With that, I stand up and say, "Well, I think I've all the information I need. I'll be heading back now to prepare your sister so we can bring her to you tomorrow," and I start walking to the front door. I open it and she's right behind me.

'"One thing more, Mr Cribb," she says.

'"Of course, Miss Holmes, what would that be?"

'"You said you would be lining the casket in white."

'"That's correct."

'She looks straight at me; her face is completely deadpan, then she says, "Do you think it would be at all possible to add a splash of purple into one of the corners? I think she would like that. She always had a wonderful sense of humour. In fact, we often used to laugh at the fact that everybody just assumed we were sisters."

'Well, you could've knocked me down with a feather, Stan, you really could. I couldn't believe what I was hearing. All those years thinking they were sodding sisters! And as she stood and told me I really think there was a slight smile hovering in the corner of her mouth. How I didn't laugh, Stan, I don't know!'

'So I then say, "Miss Holmes, I'll be more than happy to arrange for that splash of purple to be added, and I'd like to reassure you that at Cribb and Son we always respect our clients' wishes and confidence. The information you have just told me, will, and I'll give you my word, never be divulged by us."

'"I can see you are a man of honour, Mr Cribb," she says, "and I do appreciate your diplomacy. I shall see you tomorrow when you bring Eleanor home," and with that she closes the door.

'When I got in the car I had to sit there for a few minutes. I'd been completely taken aback. Christ, it did make me laugh though … all these years they've kept their secret from the gossips. Can you imagine what they would've done with that bit of news? They would've had a field day! All I thought was, good for you. I haven't laughed so much since we were in the Romford Road Baths.

175

Truthfully, Stan, I thought I'd seen and heard it all ... just goes to show!'

A short while later the bell rang, as the front door opened, and there stood Budgie. Now Budgie was an oddity, often hanging about but nobody ever knew what he did. He would creep around the streets, always dressed in the same black cap, suit and over-coat. The only splash of colour was the obli-gatory handkerchief – the colour of which I'd rather not try to describe – clamped firmly to his mouth, which he frequently coughed into. There was lots of speculation about his condition; most of the bets were on con-sumption, more commonly known as TB.

With small, pointed features, slight form, and rounded shoulders, he crept around like a small predatory animal. He was crow-like, and nothing remotely like a budgie. Nobody seemed to know the reason he was called Budgie, as he didn't dress in brightly coloured clothes or keep repeating his words, and there were no other obvious reasons. He was the type of man you would always try to avoid if you saw him before he saw you, as he always wanted something.

As he stood in the doorway, I went up to him. 'Hello, Budgie, how are you?' I asked.

'Not too bad, son. I've bin watchin' the shop. You ain't got any coppers in today, 'av ya?' was the muffled response.

'No, not today. Why you asking?' I said.

'No reason, son, no reason. Is Tom in?' he said, looking towards the back.

'Maybe I can help you, Budgie, as he's a bit busy at the moment,' I lied.

'No, son, you can't 'elp me. I've got a bit of a delicate situation only your Uncle can 'elp.' His eyes looked serious, but I couldn't see the rest of his face due to the handkerchief covering most of it.

'He's out the back. I'll go and see if he's free.' And with that I turned and walked back to the office.

Grinning, I said, 'I think this might change your mood. Budgie's outside.'

'Oh, what the hell does he want?'

'Don't know, but he says only you can help him. Apparently it's a very delicate situation.'

'Delicate, my arse! He don't know the meaning of the word; he's up to no good, that's what he's up to!'

'Good afternoon, Budgie, how are you?' said Uncle, as he walked back into the shop. 'Stan says you have a delicate situation you need to discuss with me. Now what can I do for you?'

Budgie was still half in and half out of the door but, when he heard Uncle's offer to help, he looked up and down the street then stepped in. As he shut the door behind him he held up a paper bag clutched in his hand-kerchief-free hand. 'Just got two kippers for me tea and I need somefing to cook 'em wiv,' he said.

An outlandish thought crossed my mind: I wondered how on earth he managed to eat with that handkerchief constantly clamped to his mouth, especially kippers. I mean, how did he get the bones out? They were difficult enough to eat with two hands. Just as I was pondering this thought, Uncle turned to me. 'Go upstairs and get a frying pan, Stan, big enough to cook his fish in.'

With that, he mumbled something we couldn't decipher into his handkerchief 'What'd you say?' Uncle asked.

'I said, I don't need a sodding frying pan. I need an 'ammer and screwdriver!' Then he bent over in a fit of coughing.

We both looked at one another. I shrugged, looking puzzled, whilst Uncle looked back, rolling his eyes.

'Did you say a hammer and screwdriver?' Uncle repeated, surprised.

'Yeah,' he spluttered.

'I don't get it. How you supposed to cook a pair of kippers with a hammer and screwdriver?'

'Bleeding 'ell, Tom, do I 'av to spell it out! I need the 'ammer and screwdriver to break into the sodding gas cupboard, so I can get the gas on to cook the bloody things!' Having exerted himself, he exploded into another bout of coughing.

'Now, fancy me not thinking of that! Well, you've caught me in a good mood. Go and fetch a hammer and screwdriver, Stan, we can't have those kippers going to waste now, can we!' He looked back at me as he mouthed the words 'cheap ones'. I nodded and went to fetch the tools.

Over the years, Budgie had 'borrowed' quite a number of different tools from us, so we'd learnt our lesson not to give him any of our good ones.

'Fanks,' he muttered, as I handed them over. 'I'll bring 'em back tomorra.' And off he shuffled.

'We'll never see them again,' Uncle said, as he headed back towards the office.

But I must admit he still had that smile on his face for the rest of the day.

About a week later a call came in from Mrs O'Leary. She was distraught, and, for a woman of her demeanour, it was a surprise.

Uncle answered the phone, and sat with it pulled away from his ear, as the voice coming through was hysterical.

'Now, calm down, calm down, Mrs O'Leary, don't get yourself all worked up. I'm sure your husband hasn't come back to haunt you, it's...' He then stops screwing his face up, pulling the phone even further away from his ear. *'Please calm down,* you'll do yourself no good getting this worked up. I guarantee it's the gases that have built up in his body; we'll come around right now and sort it out for you.' He pauses, listening. 'We'll see you very shortly.'

He finished the call and turned to me.

'Apparently she heard a noise from the body; it's obviously the gases but she thinks he's come back to haunt her. We'd better get over there and sort it out now before she calls in an exorcist – the woman's in a sodding frenzy!'

The front door was opened as soon as our car drew up and there she was, looking ashen, clutching her crucifix to her chest.

'Leave it to us, Mrs O'Leary, we'll sort it out for you, and I'll call you when we've finished,' Uncle said, as we walked into the front room, closing the door behind us.

The last time I'd been there was eight days previously. After that amount of time, with the weather being hot – and don't forget the candles were constantly burning morning noon and night creating even more heat in the room – you can imagine how Mr O'Leary looked. We always recommended to clients that after a few days of having the body exposed they should think about putting the coffin lid on properly, but many wouldn't listen and insisted they wanted the casket open for the duration.

I noticed that on the floor, under the coffin, was a huge bowl of chopped onions. I'd seen this many times before: it's an old wives' tale that onions are supposed to stifle the smell of the corpse, but to me it just made it a whole lot worse.

Mr O'Leary's body had blown up to such a size, it was imperative that the gases were released.

'Go on then, Stan, get on with it,' Uncle whispered, so nobody listening outside the door would hear.

I didn't like this part of the job at all, and if I could've got anyone else to do it I would've done but, as always, it was left to me.

I bent over the body and gently undid the shroud, which was tied behind, pulling it down to waist level. I then pulled out of my bag a ten-inch long metal tube; it was similar to a 'trocar', which is now used in embalming. It's hollow, with a point at the end that tapers down at the other. I pushed the sharp end into the top of the stomach, and immediately the gases started to escape. The smell! It was indescribable. It took about three minutes for them to fully release, and it was impossible to stand there for that long, as it was so overpowering. When the body had been punctured you immediately held your lighter up to the end, so the gases would then ignite, creating a flame of around two inches high. This would then burn them off, stopping the smell contaminating the room any further. Once the flame had died down, the tube would be removed, a plug placed in the hole, and the shroud put back on.

Mrs O'Leary was standing outside wringing her hands when we opened the door. 'Well?' she said. 'What's happened?'

'We've released the gases and everything's fine now, but I suggest you put the lid fully onto the casket,' Uncle said.

'No, absolutely not!' she said, shaking her head. 'He was a mean ol'bastard but I'll not have him screwed in until the day, Mr Cribb, no way!' She then added: 'And I'm still convinced he's come back to haunt me; it's just the sort of t'ing he'd do to me! I've been looking into it, so I have, and what I'd like you to do is get me a mute for the day of the funeral, and then afterwards I'm going to have the place exorcised by me priest.'

'A mute?' Uncle Tom looked at her in amazement. 'You want a mute?'

'*I certainly do!*' she said, placing her hands on her enormous hips.

I could see that Uncle Tom was not just amazed, he was shell-shocked.

'Where on earth am I supposed to get a mute from, Mrs O'Leary? Nobody's used them for the last forty-five years!'

'Well, don't you be asking me, Mr Cribb, you're the frigging undertaker. I'll be leaving it to you. I've got enough of me own problems, so I have. Now, I've to be getting on. I'll be seeing you Wednesday. I believe we're to leave at ten o'clock sharp.'

'Yes, we are. Goodbye, Mrs O'Leary, we'll see you then.'

He was furious. In the car, he turned to me. 'Having the place exorcised! I only said it as a bloody joke but she's actually going through with it, and can you believe she wants a mute? Where the hell am I going to get one of those in two days?'

Let me explain what a 'mute' is, in case you don't know. Mutes were commonplace from 1600–1914. They were usually used in pairs but sometimes singularly. They were always men, dressed completely in black, with gloves, long shrouds, and top hats with black veils attached to the back that hung down their necks onto the shoulders. They would carry a wand or staff (they were sinister-looking buggers who looked like the Grim Reaper). They would have sad, pathetic faces and would stand at the front door of the deceased's house on the morning of funerals. They were believed to ward off evil spirits and were a symbolic protector of the deceased. They wouldn't utter a word the whole time, hence the name 'mute'. When the funeral left the house they would walk in front of the cortège with the undertaker behind them, sometimes walking all the way to the cemetery, depending on the distance, or stand on the back of the horse-drawn funeral hearse.

The tradition began, apparently, when members of the aristocracy died in their large manor houses surrounded by acres of land. The houses couldn't be seen from the roadway, due to the long driveways, so a member of staff would be dressed in black and instructed to stand at the gates of the house in order to alert any passers-by that there had been a death in the house.

In Dickens's *Oliver Twist*, the undertaker Mr Sowerberry said to his wife about Oliver: *'There's an expression of melancholy in his face, my dear, which is very interesting. He would make a delightful mute, my love.'*

Let me tell you how grateful I was that I'd met Mrs O'Leary, as I knew for a fact that if I hadn't I would have definitely been dressed up by Uncle Tom to be her mute.

'You know what, Stan, I just can't believe this. The woman's definitely gone round the twist. We've already explained it's the gases, but she's convinced herself she's being haunted. Bloody hell, I bet the poor sod's glad to have got away. Why should he want to come back and haunt her? God knows what we're going to do ... put your thinking cap on, boy!'

I could see why he was worried. Two days to go and we were stuck with a considerable challenge.

We then drove back to the yard, as he wanted to check on one of the mourner's cars that had been playing up. Jack had been working on it most of the day, trying to repair it for Wednesday. As we walked over to the car we could see Jack's legs sticking out from underneath it.

'How's it looking ... had any luck?' Uncle asked, kneeling down.

Jack slid himself out, stood up, wiped his hands on an old piece of cloth and started to explain the problem. As he's doing this I could see Uncle's facial expression change: his eyes went small, his mouth started to purse, and suddenly he was deep in thought. I could see he wasn't listening to a blind word Jack was saying. I'm not looking or listening to Jack either, I'm looking at Uncle. I know the old bugger so well; something's brewing!

His eyes widen and a smile creeps on his lips. He then turns excitedly towards me, shouting, 'We've found our bloody mute, boy!'

I couldn't contain myself, and burst out laughing. I certainly wasn't expecting that! I knew by his face he was scheming but using poor Jack as the mute never entered my head. He started to chuckle and poor old Jack's left standing there looking completely bewildered, with his wonderful hangdog expression. 'What d'you mean, you've found your mute? I know I don't talk much but it's a...'

'No, no, no. It's nothing to do with you not

talking, Jack. It's your face!' Uncle says, now laughing.

'Oh, fanks,' Jack answers. 'No need to be rude!'

'Jack, you don't get it. Come with me and I'll explain everything to you.' And with that he put his arm around Jack's shoulders, leading him towards the office, winking at me as he goes.

As I stood waiting for them to come out, there was clearly a heated argument going on:

'I'm not bloody doing it!'

'Yes, you are!'

'I won't!'

'Well, don't come back then!'

You've got the gist, anyway. It went on like that for ages, and in the end Jack stormed out, grabbing his coat.

Uncle strolled over with his hands in his trouser pockets. 'No problem. He's just got to get his outfit now.'

The very next day, Mum got her sewing machine out and knocked up a black shroud and attachment to the top hat and the staff/ wand was made in the workshop.

As it turned out, Jack was the perfect 'mute' – his look and lack of speech was just what Mrs O'Leary had ordered. She was thrilled to have him standing by her front door, so all the neighbours and mourners could see. But she didn't let up for a second with her superstitions. As we started to carry the coffin out of the house she was right behind us.

'Don'tcha forget to carry him out feet first,' she hissed.

This was something we always did anyway, but she was obviously going back to the old superstition that when the deceased is carried out, it's always to be feet first, to prevent the spirit looking back into the house and beckoning another family member to follow them.

As the apprentice I always got the feet end, because if there were to be any accidents when the coffin was removed from the house, this end would take the brunt. The problem being that most of the houses we dealt with had very narrow hallways and door openings so, when we carried the coffin out from the front room into the hall, more often than not it had to be raised at the head end to get the correct angle for us to manoeuvre it. You now know the condition of these bodies ... obviously fluids had collected in the bottom of the casket, so as it was tilted these would run down and inevitably end up on my feet. I can't tell you the amount of shoes I got through during those early years. It was such a relief when I got 'promoted' to the head end.

Mr O'Leary's was a huge funeral, and it seemed like virtually all of the Irish Catholic community in the area was attending and the amount of flower tributes was incredible.

Do you remember I told you about brides needing to carry a bunch of strongly perfumed flowers to disguise their body odour? Well, that's why flowers started being brought to funerals – in order to help camouflage the smell of the body. But by modern times, like the bride, even though flowers are no longer needed for the purpose they were designed, the tradition is still followed.

After the funeral, and true to her word, Mrs O'Leary had the house exorcised the very next day.

A week or so later I was polishing a coffin in the shop when the doorbell rang. In came a poor soul, looking as poor as you could get; pathetic really. He was carrying an old sack, which looked quite heavy, and he had a resemblance to someone but I couldn't put my finger on it.

'Good morning sir, can I help you?'I asked, wiping my hands on my apron. I then held it out to shake his hand.

'Morning, son. I'm Budgie's bruvver, Sparra,' he said, taking my hand in his. It was like shaking the hand of a skeleton.

Of course! That's who he looked like!

I grinned. 'Budgie and Sparrow ... interesting names,' I said.

'Oh, don't you start!' he said. 'It's caused

embarrassment all our lives, I tell ya. Me father 'ad an obsession wiv birds, so decided to name each one of us after 'em. Bloody ridiculous. Budgie, Sparra, Robin, Dove, Linnet and Wren, that was us,' he said, shaking his head.

'Well, it's different,' I replied. 'I suppose he could've had an obsession with fish, then you would've had problems!'

He flung his head back and snorted with laughter, and I spotted one lone tooth which was rotten. 'Bloody right, son, never thought of that one. Me ol' mum always said be grateful for small mercies.'

'What can I do for you, Sparrow?'

'Came to tell ya, Budgie died last night. The consumption got 'im in the end. Lasted longer than we thought, though. Blessed release. Poor bugger was suffering in the end. Just came t' ask if you'd do 'is funeral for us, son. We've got insurance, everyfinks covered.'

'Yes, of course. I'm so sorry to hear about your brother; he certainly was a character.'

'Bloody 'ell, you can say that again,' Sparrow retorts, giving another loud snort.

We sorted out all the arrangements then, as he was leaving, he picked the sack up. 'Oh, by the way, before he died he told me this was under his bed and that 'e wanted you to 'ave it.'

'Oh, OK ... what is it?' I asked.

'Bag o' tools, son, don't know why 'e

189

wanted you to 'ave 'em though.'

I looked in the sack and all of our tools that he'd taken over the years were in there. I smiled. 'I think I do, Sparrow, thank you.'

'As long as you know what it's about, son, that'll do for me.' And with that he left.

10

Gracie
1950 (age 22)

I'd been out all morning, organising a funeral, and was looking forward to a nice sandwich and a cup of tea when, no sooner had I opened the door, Uncle shouts, 'Don't take your coat off, boy, you've another job.'

'Haven't I got time for a quick cuppa?'

'No, you haven't. Get down to Abbots Road. Wally Turpin the greengrocer died yesterday afternoon, apparently lifting a sack of spuds off his cart. His wife's waiting for you. The only reason I'm telling you to go now is that all of her kids will be at school and you'll have a bit of peace to sort things out,' he explained.

'OK, I'll get going, see you later.' And with that I turned around and headed off.

I could see his point: Mrs Turpin had thirteen children. 'Steps and stairs' we used to call them in those days, as they tended to have one a year so, if you stood them in a line, each one was just slightly taller than the next. It would certainly be easier to sort everything out if they weren't there.

I got to the front door, which was already open. I called out, 'Anyone in?' I could hear banging from inside.

'Who is it?' a woman's voice called from the back.

'It's Stan Cribb, from the undertakers,' I shouted back.

With that she peers around the hall door, wiping her hands on her apron. 'Come in, love,' she said.

'Do you want me to shut the door?' I asked.

'Na, leave it, the catch is broke and once it's shut it's 'ard to open. Gotta fix it. Wally was gonna do it but now he's...' She trailed off, lifted her apron and wiped it across her eyes. 'Can't believe it, tell ya the truth. I was just getting the tea ready while he was outside unloading his cart ... now he's gone, 'ow I'm gonna manage wiv thirteen little 'uns, God only knows!'

We walked into the sparse living room and I saw that the noise was coming from a small boy of around three years old, sitting on bare floorboards, bashing the living daylights out of a saucepan with a wooden spoon.

'Stop it, 'orace,' she shouted at the boy, who didn't take a blind bit of notice; in fact he hit it even harder. She grabbed the spoon off him, waving it in his face. 'I told you STOP IT. We can't 'ear ourselves bleeding fink, ya drivin' me round the bloody bend!' With that he gets up and walks outside.

Thank the lord for that!

'Sit down, Mr Cribb,' she said, pointing to one of the two rickety wooden chairs placed either side of an old table. It was a common sight to see houses so sparsely furnished. When you had that amount of children, putting food into their mouths was more important than furniture. I knew that upstairs the children would all be sharing a couple of beds between them; they would sleep like sardines, top to tail, many of them infested with fleas.

'Thank you, now let me get my paperwork out and we can get everything sorted.'

Just as I'd pulled it from my bag, a commotion starts outside in the backyard. Horace walks back in with a duck under his arm, which he can hardly carry. He walks up to me, grinning, and the duck goes into a frenzy and starts fighting to get out of his grip. Horace lets it go, and suddenly it's flapping and quacking around the living room.

The mother shouts, 'Get that thing out! How many times do I 'ave to tell you to keep the duck out of 'ere!'

It finds its own way outside and Horace is now standing next to me, just staring. It's unsettling, as he's got a strange look in his eyes as if he's deciding what he can do next to cause havoc, but at least he's quiet. I look at him and smile. A trail of something truly revolting is leaking from his nose, and I wanted to gag when his mother says, 'Wipe ya nose, 'orace, it's disgusting!' With that he wipes his sleeve right across it, spreading it over his face; his eyes never leave mine, as if he's mesmerised.

I certainly wasn't mesmerised. I couldn't bear to look any longer. I could feel the muscles in my face had fixed into a look of revulsion and I didn't want Mrs Turpin to see it. God only knows what it was like when the other twelve were there.

'If you don't behave, 'orace, you know what you'll get!' she threatened. At least this broke his trance-like state.

'No!' Horace shouted, turning to glare at her.

'You wait and see then, I've warned ya,' she said, shaking her finger at his face.

Horace ran off towards the backyard again, and this threat, whatever it was, had seemed to work, so we carried on.

I had explained virtually everything to her and was just finishing up the paperwork when I heard a clip-clop coming from behind me. I turned around and saw Horace leading a donkey into the room. I wasn't sure what I should do, as Mrs Turpin didn't seem overly concerned, so I just carried on talking. Then it was behind me, hot breath on the back of my neck, and my hair being ruffled by its lips. I sat forwards to get away from it when Mrs Turpin says, 'Don't worry, she's alright, Mr Cribb, it's only Gracie, Wally's donkey. He used to go out with 'er every day on the cart. He was with 'er before he met me. They've been together for donkeys' years.' She paused. 'You know what? I'd laugh at that if it wasn't so bloody tragic! I think she knows what's 'appened, look at 'er little face, she's so sad.'

I looked at her face but I couldn't tell. Donkeys always looked sad to me. I didn't want to upset her, so I agreed. 'Yes, I see what you mean. I can see there's sadness in her eyes.'

'That's exactly what I thought,' she said, pleased that she'd thought I'd noticed.

With that, Gracie laid her head on my shoulder.

'Aw, look!' she says. 'She taken to ya. Give 'er a little scratch on 'er nose, she likes that.'

So I there scratching Gracie's nose while I continued finalising the arrangements. Horace, now bored that his introduction of the donkey hadn't caused pandemonium, wandered off again.

As I was scratching her nose I heard an enormous rumble coming from the donkey's belly. You could sense she was uncomfortable, the way she shifted; she started lifting her back leg up as if she wanted to reach her stomach, and you could see she was distressed. Her stomach was now gurgling, and it was disturbingly loud. Her tail was swishing backwards and forwards. Something was brewing in there and I didn't like the signs one bit!

'Calm down, Gracie!' Mrs Turpin said. 'She's upset, Mr Cribb, that's what it is.'

'I know a bit about animals, Mrs Turpin. She seems to be having a problem with her stomach. It's as if she's got the gripes or something.' I was trying to warn her.

'Gripes? She can't 'ave the gripes! She hasn't eaten anything different. No, it's not that,' she replied, looking the donkey over.

Just then, Horace walks back in, the contents of his nose now dried all over his face. Walking up to Gracie, he holds out his hand and commences to feed her, but I can't make out what it is.

'What ya been giving 'er, ya little sod?' his mother shouts.

'Nuffink!' the delightful Horace shouts back, jumping up and down clapping his hands.

'You've given 'er something ... now what is it?' she screams.

Gracie is now extremely agitated and prancing up and down like she's on hot coals.

Horace skips outside and comes back holding a packet. He hands it to his mother, whose hand shoots up to her mouth as she lets out a stifled scream.

'Dear God in 'eaven!' She's now looking

panic-stricken. 'Have you given her the whole sodding packet?'

'Yeah ... all gone!' Horace laughs, opening his hands.

She grabs his hands, pulling him towards her. 'When did you give 'em to 'er?'

'She liked 'em, 'ad 'em for breakfast,' he answered, still laughing.

'Breakfast!' She quickly looks around at the mantelpiece clock. 'That was six hours ago!' She looked horrified.

'What's he given her, Mrs Turpin?' I asked, leaning forward trying to see what was on the packet.

'Senna pods!' she screams, holding up the packet to show me.

I don't think in my entire life I'd ever moved so fast.

I grabbed my papers under my arm; I didn't even stop to put them in my bag.

'Well, I think we've finished everything, Mrs Turpin, I'd better be off now.' I turned to Horace. 'Cheerio, Horace, be a good boy for your mum.'

The little sod only turns and gives me the 'soldiers' farewell'. At least, I think it was; it could have been the 'V' for Victory sign and he was too young to realise he'd got it the wrong way around but, knowing Horace, I think he knew exactly what he was doing.

If you don't know what the 'soldiers' fare-well' is, it's the two-finger salute. You wouldn't think a child of that age would know such things, would you?

I shot out of the room like greased lighting, having had many years of suffering at the hands of the senna pod, I knew by the way Gracie was behaving exactly what was coming and it was imminent.

As I reached the front door, which was fortunately open, I heard Mrs Turpin shouting to Horace: 'Get 'er out of 'ere now ... quick ... go on!'

I managed to get to the pavement when I heard a scream, followed by Mrs Turpin's cry of 'Gawd almighty!' followed by Horace's hysterical laughter.

I stood there listening to her yelling at Horace. I was guilt-ridden. I'd left her right at the critical moment but knew there was nothing I could've done to have stopped what I imagined to be Gracie's enormous expulsion. I did feel sorry for her. Not only had she just lost her husband but she now had to clear her living room of half a ton of donkey diarrhoea.

The funeral was held the following week. Mr Turpin had left specific instructions that Gracie was to pull the cart that took his coffin to the church. We made arrangements that we would take him most of the way in the hearse with Gracie (who had now fully recovered) and the cart waiting by the cemetery gates would take him the rest of the way. The cart had been beautifully decorated with wild flowers that the family had picked, as they couldn't afford anything else, and Gracie looked far perkier than the last time I'd seen her. It seemed that being 'purged' had done her the power of good. In fact, she looked a picture. Her head halter had been entwined with daisies, which his daughters had created, and his eldest son Cyril led the procession up to the church.

They were absolutely delightful children; all dressed in their Sunday best, they were a credit to their parents. Cyril told me he'd now taken over his father's business and his brother, Alf, who was fifteen, had secured a job as a runner in the docks. I was relieved; at least their mother would now have their wages to help her along. Fortunately there was no sign of Horace. I was told he was at home being looked after by a neighbour ... all I could think was *God help them!*

Animals were a common sight in a lot of households. As I explained before, they were normally kept for food but the 'totters' – who were rag and bone men, greengrocers, knife grinders – all of these professions would keep a donkey or pony to pull their carts.

When I married Joan on 17 November 1950, our house turned into a menagerie too, and that was well before our three children,

Graham, John and Susan came along.

Mum and Dad had decided to retire to the Isle of Wight, to live in my paternal grandfather's old house, so I was then able to buy our old house from them.

Dad had left a couple of chickens for us but we decided to buy a few more. I contacted a breeder in Alton Hampshire, and ordered twelve Rhode Island Reds. They were about sixteen weeks old and at the 'point of lay', which meant we only had to wait around two to three weeks for them to start supplying us with eggs. This is something I'd always wanted to do ever since I was a boy. It was all very exciting!

Over the course of the next few years, I had twenty-four Rhode Island Reds, twelve Barton's Miniatures, and a few Cuckoo Marans, that laid the most unusual chocolate-brown eggs.

Joan's dad worked with a Dutch antique dealer in town, and in conversation one day he told him about our smallholding. When he mentioned the unusual chickens with their oddly coloured eggs, he became quite emotional. The dealer explained to him that when he was a boy his father had kept Cuckoo Marans, and he'd always remembered the wonderful flavour of their eggs and he'd not had another since those days.

Joan's dad took him half a dozen as a gift and, the following day, he told him that while eating them for his tea, all his childhood memories had come flooding back. He said he'd found them delicious and he'd happily pay £1 for a regular order of a dozen per fortnight. Now, for somebody to pay £1 for a dozen eggs in those days was astonishing!

In October we'd buy in around twenty capons, to get them ready for Christmas. Capons are actually cockerels that have been doctored by injecting a small pellet into their necks. This stops them having any sexual urges, so they stop breeding and, fortunately, it stops them from crowing, too, which the neighbours certainly appreciated. Their only interest in life is to eat, which they quite happily do all day. This fattens them up so, by Christmas, you have a chicken which is very similar in size to a small turkey. Joan and I used to prepare a capon, a rabbit and half-a-dozen eggs in a basket, which sold like hot cakes at Christmas.

Having spent two years on the farm, Joan was a dab hand at preparing the animals for food. I must confess that she used to 'draw' them too (this is cleaning them out, but I could never bring myself to do it). Slaughtering, plucking, skinning – not a problem, but drawing I just couldn't do; it made me feel ill. She used to take the micky out of me all the time over that. I suppose she was right in a way. It always puzzled me how I could do what I did all day and not bring myself to 'draw' a rabbit.

Of an evening, I used to love sitting at the dining-room table going over my books. It was a good job Uncle never saw me, as he would've definitely thought I'd turned from Uriah Heep into Ebenezer Scrooge. After a few years, our smallholding in our tiny garden was almost making more profit than the undertakers!

What made life even more arduous was rationing, and it would last another four years. It was such a testing time for mothers, who had to try and feed their families on the meagre portions handed out by the government. Trying to plan weekly meals was a mission in itself, but I think having us there to provide the odd chicken, rabbit or half-a-dozen eggs made life a bit easier for them.

We even had rationing books for the animal feed too – that's how hard it was. But because the neighbours were so keen for us to keep going, they would always leave their potato peelings and scraps wrapped in newspaper on our doorstep, which I'd then turn into feed for the chickens. If it hadn't been for all those scraps I doubt we could've carried on. Everybody tried to help each other out. They were tough old days but the team spirit was remarkable.

As Charles Dickens said: *'It was the best of times, it was the worst of times…'*

11

The Great Smog
1952 (age 24)

I will never forget 1952 for two reasons: our first child Graham was born in the January and, secondly, it turned out to be the year when 'The Great Smog' engulfed us. Both events are indelibly imprinted on my memory.

As I left the house the morning of 6 December 1952 I'd picked up the hurricane lamp I used at night to go and check on our menagerie. Why I'd picked it up I don't know, but subconsciously it must have had something to do with the thick fog or 'pea-souper' that had started the previous day.

Us British had been used to bouts of fog over the years; since Roman times we were famous the world over for our mists and fog and it was rumoured that tourists even took jars of it home with them. Records dating back to the 13th century recognised that air pollution was a public health problem, and the burning of coal was the main source. Around 1807 our smoke-laden capital came known as a 'London particular' and Charles

Dickens used the term in his novel *Bleak House*, where he describes fog-bound London. Robbers in those times loved the density of it, as it allowed them to seek out travellers who had become disorientated and lost their way, making them easy-pickings.

Robbers might have loved it, but in the early 1950s a certain undertaker was cursing the weather. Uncle had picked me up to attend a funeral in Leytonstone; stupidly I'd tried to sneak the lamp into the hearse, but it was a waste of time trying to do anything without his beady eyes seeing it. 'What you bringing that thing with you for?' he said, puzzled.

'I don't know, just thought we may need it if the fog thickens up.'

'Daft bugger, it won't get any worse than this,' he said. But little did we know the events over the next five days would prove to be the worst peacetime catastrophe of the twentieth century, and would become known as 'The Great Smog'.

We went to St Patrick's Church in Leytonstone and the funeral went without a hitch. We had one hearse and one limousine for the family. We left the cemetery and were travelling along Leytonstone High Road and had just reached Maryland Point when it engulfed us, and not only us, but London as a whole. We had never witnessed anything like it. It was as if someone had set fire to a heap of tyres and let them burn – it was that black, and not only that, the smell was awful, sickening, like rotten eggs.

Freezing conditions had hit us that winter of '52. Everyone had coal fires and families were keeping them stoked up all the time, as their homes were so cold. The soot from all the chimneys and of course the factories, which daily belched out 1,000 tonnes of smoke, combined with the fog was how the word 'smog' came about. The smoke was made up of 2,000 tonnes of carbon dioxide, 140 tonnes of hydrochloric acid, 14 tonnes of fluorine compounds and 370 tonnes of sulphur dioxide. These became a deadly cocktail and, when mixed with the moisture in the air, 800 tonnes of sulphuric acid was formed.

Let me try to describe what it was like. Imagine if you held your hands out in front of you and they disappeared – that's how thick it was. It was horrible and filthy. It killed 900 people a day during those five days, 4,000 in that first week, 8,000 in the following fortnight and around 12,000 in total. It was black and evil and crept silently under doors and through windows and suffocated you in your sleep. Within a few days, undertakers all over London, including us, had run out of coffins and were working as hard as they could under dire conditions to make as many as was physically possible.

We stopped the cars. It was impossible to go any further but we had to try and get back to the yard, otherwise we knew we'd be there all night. We had covered our mouths and noses with scarves, as you felt like choking if it hit the back of your throat. We sat in silence, racking our brains as to what we could do. I remember sitting there, thinking, How the hell are we going to get out of this? But I'm pleased to say Uncle's thoughts were far more imaginative than mine.

'Right! Get the broom out the back, Stan,' he said, suddenly motivated. We always kept a broom in the back of the hearse to sweep up flower petals after each casket had been removed. I went and fetched it. Then he ordered me to 'take off the brush', which I did. You all know by now why I didn't question what he was up to.

'Now, light up that hurricane lamp you pushed in the back this morning.' I'm glad I had the scarf around my face because I couldn't contain a grin.

'Here's the plan. Tommy, you walk in the gutter holding one end of the handle and the lamp. I'll walk next to the car holding the other end and the car door handle. Stan, open the window a bit so you can hear us and you drive. Charlie's driving behind, so we need two of the gentlemen mourners to help us out. Take off your coat, Tommy,' he ordered.

'Bloody hell, it's freezing guv, I'll catch me deaf if I get a chill in me kidneys.'

I took a breath and closed my eyes in anticipation.

'If you still want a job in the morning,' he yelled, 'you'll GET THAT SODDING COAT OFF NOW!'

I've never seen a coat taken off so quickly. 'Here you are, guv, all yours,' he simpered. I smiled again – at least for once it wasn't me on the receiving end.

Uncle then crept back to the car behind and explained to the two mourners what he wanted them to do. His idea was that one would walk at the front wing of their car and one at the rear of our car, holding the coat between them, so they could judge where each other was. It wasn't perfect, but we didn't have a lot of options.

With everybody organised and in position we started off. I couldn't see Uncle Tom, let alone Tommy; all I could see was the faint glimmer of the lamp. We were hardly moving; it was unbelievably frightening – nothing but complete blackness all around us. We crawled along; literally inching our way along the road. It was virtually impossible to see anything through the windscreen, as big flakes of greasy soot stuck on the glass. I couldn't wipe it off so I wound the window down and put my head out. After several hours we'd managed to reach East London

Cemetery in Plaistow, when all of a sudden I saw a flickering red light – a trolley bus. I have never felt so excited to see a trolley bus in all my life!

'Quickly ... Uncle ... Tommy, get in! There's a trolley bus up ahead. I can see the red light, we can follow that,' I shouted.

Uncle relayed the news to the mourners, who were walking at the rear, and headed back to their car. Tommy was instructed to hang his arm out of the window holding onto my lamp, so they could try and keep us in view as we sped up.

'You're going too bloody fast, boy!' Uncle shouted.

I couldn't tell you how relieved I was to see the bus. 'There it is can you see it?' I yelled excitedly. 'We're almost up to it!'

Then there was one almighty crash, and we all shot forward onto the dashboard. A second later, a smash to the rear knocked us all backwards.

'I've done me neck in!' Tommy shouted.

'You've run into the back of the trolley bus, you bloody idiot,' said Uncle. 'I said you were going too fast! Get out and see what's going on!' He was roaring now – and you all know what happens when he roars.

I jumped out to check the damage; the one good thing about the smog was that it concealed my Uriah Heep impersonation.

When I reached the front of the car I was

expecting to see the bus, but what I found was the Beaconsfield Public House covered in scaffolding, with a flickering lamp attached to it and our car imbedded into it. I stood there, assessing the damage. The car was crushed in at the front, but the scaffolding wasn't damaged at all, so there was some good news – we wouldn't have to pay out for somebody else's repairs. But I knew the fact that I had mistaken a pub with scaffolding around it for a trolley bus would never be able to counteract my piece of 'good news'.

As I stood there, a little voice in my head screamed, 'Run away! Go on, go! Nobody will see you. GO!'

Even though I wanted to run, I couldn't. I was twenty-four, I had been to war, for heaven's sake. I was a man! I had to stand up and take the rap. I swallowed hard. 'Oh, dear God, *please* help me. I'm going to get hung, drawn and quartered.'

I was then shaken out of my thoughts.

'Stan, what the hell's going on?' Uncle yelled. 'We can't see a thing. Is the trolley bus driver with you?'

I walked back. 'Er ... no, it's er ... just me. It's not a trolley bus at all, it's ... scaffolding,' I muttered behind my scarf.

'It's what?' he roared. 'Speak up, what's the matter with you, boy!' I pulled the scarf away from my mouth. 'I said, it's not a trolley bus. It's scaffolding.'

'SCAFFOLDING! We've hit scaffolding. I don't bloody believe it!' He jumped out of the car and made his way to the front. I followed as he bent down to inspect the damage, muttering under his scarf. He then quickly stood up, turned and grabbed the lapels of my overcoat, and started shaking me backwards and forwards, screaming, 'You're a sodding simpleton, Stan, that's what you are. A sodding simpleton! WHAT ARE YOU?'

'A sodding simpleton, Uncle,' I replied in rhythm to his shakes, and this time I really had to agree with him.

After my public humiliation, we managed to get the cars started and carried on the way we had before the doomed 'trolley bus' sighting. We got back to the yard about forty-five minutes later, but the nightmare wasn't over, as we all then had to venture out again in order to find our way home.

It took me another wretched two hours to get home. I came across people in the street completely disorientated, and cars had been left abandoned. It wasn't too bad while you were on the main roads, but when I say it wasn't too bad I mean that the visibility varied from between eight to five feet. When you left the main road to walk down the side streets, that's when it dropped to about a foot. It was horrible, as the atmosphere felt sinister, and the blackness and silence made it unsettlingly eerie.

People were hanging onto the privet hedges that lined the front of the houses, working their way along the street inch by inch, counting the houses until they came to their own. But if you lost count you would then have to feel for the number on the front gate or walk up to a front door and try to find which number you were at before carrying on. It was such a relief when you actually did get home.

But even when you got inside you could still see it in your rooms, hovering like the deadly spectre it was, leaving a thick film of black dust in its wake; there was no escaping it.

I couldn't believe it when I looked in the hall mirror – my hair was thick with black grease and my face, from my red, sore eyes up, was full of oily black smudges.

You would meet people whose lips were actually blue. They wouldn't survive for very long; their lungs had been inflamed by breathing in the foul, toxic air and they were slowly suffocating to death. You've heard the saying 'dead man walking', well that was them; you were literally meeting the living dead. Hospitals were rapidly filling up, and where patients thought they could escape the smog in those safe surroundings they shockingly discovered it had infiltrated the wards and the corridors of the hospitals too. No matter where you went it followed. More than 100,000 people were afflicted with health problems after that dreadful week, and heaven only knows the amount that suffered a premature death later on because of it.

Not only did it affect every person in the East End, and also parts of Central and South London, it also impacted on farming communities who had filled Smithfield market with cattle to be sold and slaughtered for food. Some collapsed, gasping for air and many animals had to be destroyed, as their lungs had been so badly infected they had turned black and were deemed inedible.

Over the next few days, London virtually came to a standstill. Headlines read: The Great Smog grows worse; death toll rises; London paralysed, no buses, taxis, coaches, trains or planes; Hospitals full to bursting.

When it cleared, thankfully due to a wind that picked up, it left every building, plant and tree looking as if they'd been sprayed with an oily black residue. Although it took weeks, the rain eventually washed it away, and as it did so the gutters flowed with vile-smelling filth.

For every person who lived through those dreadful five days, their memories will be as grim as the smog itself.

12

Lily
1955 (age 27)

As I told you before, I kept Cuckoo Maran chickens and sold a dozen of their eggs every fortnight for £1. I sometimes wished if I'd had a chicken coop full of them, *plus* £1 a time for every person whose asked me about embalming, I would be a very wealthy man.

Embalming is a fascination for many people; there's a morbid curiosity that surrounds it. We started using it during the mid-1950s, as it was just catching on then in our part of the world. We had no training, so we employed the services of Lear Embalming Co., who were based in Carshalton. They were George and Josephine – a husband and wife team. The process at that time could be carried out in several places: our workshop in Ford Street, the hospital mortuary – if a post mortem had been required – or it could even be done in the home of the bereaved.

It took quite a time to take off. As I said, people just didn't know what to expect. The most common reaction when it was offered to them was 'No thanks, I don't like the idea of it' or We don't want them to be cut up.' I would then explain that there wasn't any cutting-up involved. If the body had been autopsied, that's when you could say that it had been 'cut-up', but the embalming process required only several small incisions to enable the preservation liquid to be introduced into the body. It was in fact originally known as 'temporary preservation'.

You remember the story about Mr O'Leary and how his body had blown up full of gases, and how it leaked liquids in the decomposition process? Well, that was the norm in those days, as there wasn't an alternative. It was a traumatic experience for the mourners to see their loved ones decompose in front of their eyes, so embalming stopped all of these processes and allowed them to view the body for their final goodbyes whilst remaining in virtually perfect condition.

There is another skill attached to this too, which is the cosmetic side, and it can also be a great help in the reconstruction of heads and faces. If the person has been involved in an accident, it enables the family to see them once again before the funeral takes place, which certainly wouldn't have been advisable beforehand.

Embalming has been around for thousands of years. It started in Ancient Egypt with the mummies but it became more widely available to the public in America. It started to be used more frequently during the American Civil War, which started in 1861. Dr Thomas Holmes – known as 'the Father of American embalming' – was engaged by the medical department of the Union Army to set up battlefield embalming stations, to enable the bodies of soldiers to be returned home in the best condition possible.

The kind of fluids used was a trade secret but arsenic was the primary agent. This is highly poisonous, so it killed or stopped the microorganisms in the body that caused decomposition.

You can imagine how dangerous it was, using this highly toxic substance to perform an embalming. Any trace of the arsenic may have been digested in some way by the embalmers; this would result in their death, so being an embalmer was not a sought-after profession.

The other problem was that, throughout the 1880s, embalming had become increasingly popular, but over time the wooden caskets would degrade, which then allowed the remains, that were full of arsenic, to be exposed to the earth that entombed them. This resulted in entire cemeteries becoming hazardous, as the ground and any surrounding water supplies, wells, rivers etc., became toxic due to the release of so much poison.

Fortunately, in the early 1900s, arsenic

was banned, due to concern for the health of the embalming practitioners and the contamination of land. The fluid now used is formaldehyde.

It was mid-afternoon when I took a call from an extremely distressed man; I could barely make out what he was saying.

'My daughter was ... killed this morning.' I then heard sobbing on the other end and gasps for breath. After a short while he said, 'I'm sorry.'

'Don't worry, sir, take all the time you need. I'm here when you're ready.' I sat with the phone against my ear and continued listening to him crying. 'Would it be easier if I came around to see you?'I suggested.

He blew his nose and sniffed. 'Could you? It would be ... better, I think.'

'Of course, what's your name and address?' I asked.

'Tony Rickwood. Wilson Road. East Ham.'

'I'll be there in about half an hour.'

'Who was that, boy?' Uncle called from the office.

'A Mr Rickwood from Wilson Road, sounds absolutely devastated. Said his daughter was killed this morning.'

'Poor devil. D'you want me to go? It'll be a tough one.'

'No, it's alright. I'll go, but thanks for offering. I'll take the van, if that's OK?'I said, grabbing my overcoat, hat and scarf, as it was a bitterly cold day.

'Of course. I'm not planning on going anywhere. I'll see you later,' he said, turning back to his account books.

I pulled up outside a very attractive little house and knocked on the front door. My breath came out as white steam, as I blew onto my frozen hands. It took quite a while to open and when it was I was shocked by the appearance of the man. His face was puffed up and blotchy with crying, and he was physically shaking. There's absolutely nothing you can do in a situation like that, even after years and years of experience. It's impossible to know what to say when you are confronted with such extreme grief.

'Good afternoon, Mr Rickwood. Stan Cribb ... you called me a while ago.'

'Yes, come in, go through,' he said, pointing towards the living room.

I walked in and heard him close the door behind me. In the living room a woman was lying on the settee sobbing into a cushion. 'I told you, I don't want to see anyone, Tony. I just can't,' said the muffled voice.

'It's the undertaker, love. We have to sort it out, we can't put it off,' he said softly.

'I can't. I just can't!' she said, and pushed her face deeper into the cushion.

'Please sit down, Mr Cribb. Can I get you a cup of tea or something?'

'No, thank you, I'm fine.' I smiled as I sat down.

He then sat down at the end of the settee next to his wife. 'Our daughter Lily was killed. She was run over outside school this morning.' He paused to wipe his eyes, whilst his wife sobbed, trying to cover her ears at the same time.

'She was only twelve ... our only child ... an angel, she was.' He shook as he gulped in a breath of air.

'I'm so *very* sorry. I just wish I could say something to ease your pain but I know nothing I say will be of any help. But I do understand how difficult this is for you.' I paused for a second. 'I think the best thing I can do for you right now is to sort out the arrangements as quickly as possible, then I can get out of your way and leave you in peace.'

'Yes, yes, let's sort it quickly, if you don't mind. Let's just get it done. I've been dreading it,' he said, wiping his eyes with the back of his hand.

His wife slowly sat up. She looked as if she hadn't an ounce of strength left in her.

'I want to see her ... *please* can I see her?' she asked pitifully, her voice a dry croak.

I looked at her husband, hoping he would help me out, as I didn't know what she meant.

'You know you can't see her, love. They

said it wasn't a good idea,' he said, as he put his arm around her.

'But I want to ... I *have* to! I need to say goodbye. I never had a chance.'

Mr Rickwood looked at me. 'Lily was badly injured ... her head ... they said we shouldn't identify her, that somebody else should do it. My brother-in-law's a policeman, and he did it. We just wanted to see her again ... as she was ... it doesn't seem right not being able to say goodbye.' He trailed off, pulling his wife into his chest.

'I understand. Anybody in your position would feel exactly the same.' I paused, leaning forward. 'But you know, there *are* things that can be done now, marvellous things which may help you to see Lily again,' I said encouragingly.

It's very hard trying to contain your emotions when you're witnessing this type of sorrow. I never ever got used to it but I learned to control it. At times like this people are at their weakest emotionally and they need to know someone is there to take responsibility and to help them through it.

Both of them looked towards me in unison. Mrs Rickwood spoke first. 'There's a way we can see her ... how? Oh *please* don't get our hopes up. I don't think I could bear it!' she said, wringing her hands. Her husband took one of her hands in his. 'Do you mean it?' he asked.

'Yes I do,' I said.

'But how?'

'Well, if you agree to have her embalmed...' I started to explain.

'NO!' screamed Mrs Rickwood, her hands shooting up to cover her face. 'She's been through enough. You're not going to cut her up. You can't, I won't let you!'

'Wait, love, let's hear what Mr Cribb has to say first,' her husband said, looking at me and nodding to carry on.

'I know of a company who specialises in this type of thing. They're experts in recon-struction. I've seen some of their work, and it's quite remarkable. I believe that if I got them to look at Lily they'd be able to make her look the way she used to.'

'Would they be able to make her look *exactly* as she was?' he said.

'I think they would get very close,' I said confidently.

'Could she ... come back home?' his wife said.

'Yes, once everything's been done we can bring her back here, if that's what you would like.'

They didn't know what to do; their emotions were running so high, they weren't even aware this type of reconstruction work existed. They needed time to think, so I took the rest of the details and left them to decide.

I hadn't been back in the shop more than thirty minutes explaining to Uncle what had happened when the phone rang.

'Mr Cribb, it's Mr Rickwood. We've decided we want Lily to come home, looking ... as she did...' His voice was a quiver.

'I'm so happy you've made that decision. I'll contact the company now and get everything organised. I would think we're talking about a week or so, as there has to be a coroner's report before they release Lily. That will take at least three days and then it may be another two or three days after that before I can bring her home, but I'll let you know,' I said.

'I'll wait to hear, then, and thank you,' he said, hanging up.

I got straight onto the company and explained the situation. They were prepared to come and take a look at Lily after the case was cleared by the coroner's court.

I'd put myself well and truly on the line, as we'd never done anything like it before. All I could do now was pray that it would be a success.

Lily had to be autopsied as, even though it seemed clear cut that she'd slipped on the icy road running to get to school, and had fallen under the wheels of a tram, it had to be confirmed that it was in fact a tragic road traffic accident, and not the result of a heart attack, haemorrhage or some other reason.

Autopsies are always used where there is a sudden death, such as a murder, road accident or where a GP isn't able to accurately state the cause of death. It normally took around three days for the report to reach the coroner, who would then decide if the case could be closed or left open for more witness statements to be collected and studied.

Professor Keith Simpson was the Home Office Pathologist at that time. A genius in his field, he was one of the original forensic pathologists. When he worked on a murder case his findings could hang a man or free him; he was revolutionary for his time. He arrived at the West Ham Mortuary, where Lily had been taken, to perform the autopsy. I was there when he arrived, dressed impeccably in his bowler hat and three-piece suit. He was accompanied by an extremely attractive woman in a fur hat and coat. They both entered the mortuary. A while later, just as I was preparing to leave, I noticed the mortuary door had been left slightly ajar. I could hear a clicking sound coming from inside. I couldn't resist taking a peek, and crept up to stare through the crack in the door. There he was, bent over Lily, his jacket removed and replaced by an apron, but still firmly placed on his head was his bowler hat. Sitting on the opposite side of the room was his secretary, still in her fur hat, typing up his report on her portable typewriter.

His report was later forwarded to the Coroner's Office, and it was clear from the results and the statements taken from the eye witnesses that this was an accident. She had been a perfectly healthy twelve-year-old but on that freezing morning fate had cruelly intervened and her young life was tragically lost.

After the hearing I made another visit to see Mr and Mrs Rickwood. I needed a recent photo of Lily, so the reconstruction team could recreate her to as near a likeness as possible. When I told them she would be back in three days, they were thrilled. I know it sounds odd when you say words like thrilled, but they were getting their daughter back when they thought they would never be able to see her again.

When they started work she had in fact been dead for five days. I had been concerned that she would have started to decompose while we waited for the reports to be completed. Chiller units in which to keep bodies had yet to become available. But luckily the weather had been bitterly cold over that week, so the body had been well-preserved.

Firstly she was embalmed, and then they spent three days working on her head and face. It was painstaking but the end result was fantastic, and you would never have known that she'd sustained any injury. They were masters of their craft, and I often thought what a wonderful skill it was to be able to bring a person who'd been so badly injured back to their families looking the way they did before. The satisfaction from accomplishing that type of work must have been so rewarding.

When Lily was ready, I delivered her back home; we carried her in and placed her casket on two easels in the front room. Her mum and dad stayed in the back room until she was settled. I then called them in.

They stood at the door threshold, Mr Rickwood's arm around his wife's shoulder; they looked as if they had aged twenty years.

As they both walked tentatively forward they were not looking into the coffin. Mr Rickwood was staring straight ahead, and his wife's head was buried into his neck, her left hand clutching onto his shirt.

He looked first. I'd never heard such an intake of breath. 'Oh, my God! My sweet girl...' His voice trailed off and he stood with tears streaming down his face. Then his wife opened her eyes and looked up at him. 'Tony, I can't look, I *just can't!*' she sobbed, her knuckles turning white as her hand clenched and unclenched on his chest.

'She's beautiful, Jean, please look, it's alright, *really* it is.'

She slowly turned her head to look down. As her eyes reached her daughter, her hand shot to her mouth. 'Oh, Tony!' she said, looking up at her husband. 'I can't believe it. I just can't believe it, our beautiful baby ... she's here!' She stroked her daughter's jet-black hair. 'Oh, Lily, darling. darling Lily. We've missed you so much.' She stood there for a few minutes, staring as if hypnotised.

I gently cleared my throat. I knew they'd forgotten I was there. 'I'll make my own way out,' I said softly.

Mrs Rickwood was in a world of her own and my speaking had jarred her from her thoughts. She dragged her gaze away. 'Oh I'm *so* sorry, Mr Cribb, it's just that I can't believe it!' She then took my hand. 'We can't thank you enough, can we, Tony,' she said, looking around at him. 'We never thought we'd see her again but you brought her back to us as you said you would. Thank you, thank you *so much*.' And she turned back to look at her daughter.

I left them both standing by the coffin. I wouldn't have been surprised to hear that they'd stayed in that room together for the remaining days before the funeral was held; they looked to me as if they would've been happy to stay there forever. I couldn't have been happier with the outcome. The Rickwoods had got their lovely daughter back to say their goodbyes.

It had been my first embalming and reconstruction, but it certainly wouldn't be my last. So many people heard the news about Lily that their negative thoughts about embalming changed overnight.

On the beautiful wreath of lilies that Mr and Mrs Rickwood placed on top of their daughter's casket, the card read:

A beautiful flower, lent not given, to bud on earth and bloom in heaven.

13

A New Start
1955 (age 27)

'Good morning, Uncle,' I said cheerfully, as I walked through the shop door one morning. I'd been on holiday to the Isle of Wight for a fortnight with Joan, who was now expecting our second child. We'd had a wonderful time visiting my parents, who were thoroughly enjoying their retirement. I was feeling very relaxed and happy to be back at work.

'I'll take your word for it, boy,' he answered, as he looked up at me from reading his morning *Daily Sketch*.

I wanted to say, 'Well, aren't we full of the joys of spring?' But I didn't.

It was funny, really. I was in my late twenties, we'd worked together for thirteen years, and yet I still had to watch how I spoke to him. I wouldn't have dared to say something like that, as I would've been scared stiff of his response. Nephew or not, I knew he wouldn't have any hesitation in sacking me. But as children we were always taught to be respectful of our elders. Even if you didn't agree with them you would never have dreamt of answering them back, or being 'lippy'.

So all I said was, 'How's business been?' as I sat down opposite him.

'Not turned a wheel since you been gone,' he said looking concerned.

'What! Not one funeral in over two weeks?' I was amazed.

'No, not even an enquiry ... nothing. God knows what we're going to do.'

'What can we do? We'll just have to ride it out. It's got to turn around,' I said encouragingly.

But it didn't; in fact it got much worse.

During one month we held only two funerals. Uncle and I were going without wages in order that the staff would be able to take some money home. Things were dire, and how we didn't go under heaven only knows. Thank goodness I still had my smallholding to help supplement us.

I've no doubt the problem was caused by so many people being killed during the war or having been made homeless, deciding they would take the opportunity to move away rather than stay in the area.

When you think of the devastation the war caused you can understand why there was such a shortage of people. In the first five months of the Blitz in the London area alone 33,757 houses had been bombed beyond repair, 123,395 were seriously damaged, but were able to be repaired, and 379,140 had been damaged but needed smaller repairs. The Ministry of Home Security was in charge and everything was paid for out of the 'War Fund'. They estimated it would cost them £750 (equivalent to around £30,000 in today's money) to rebuild a destroyed house, £100 for the major damage to be repaired and £30 for minor damage. Now this is the amazing part: the total bill had in that short time already reached £113,115,390 and we still had months and months of heavy bombing raids to endure. It's remarkable how the country survived with that debt, let alone our small business. After two horrendous years, towards the end of 1947, things had gradually started to turn around. It had been an incredibly hard time, putting all of us under immense pressure.

After the New Year, I knew I had to sit down with Tom and discuss where we were going with the business. I hated the thought of these 'chats', as he was such a difficult man to talk to, especially as he grew older. He just wouldn't deal with things and I would become frustrated with his lack of communication. To tell you the God's honest truth, it got me down so much that sometimes I went home and wept into my pillow. I know it sounds weak on my part, but I had so much respect for him and, as I said, to answer back or be confrontational just wasn't an option, so I had to deal with it in my own way.

It's peculiar, isn't it, how you live with certain things for years and years then one day everything looks different? You can't explain why, but all of a sudden you've noticed it. That's exactly what happened to me.

I was outside the shop this particular morning, rooted to the spot, staring at the front. I'd got so used to seeing it, I didn't notice it any more. I studied it closely. How in heaven's name had it stayed standing for so long? It was literally on the verge of collapse.

It hadn't been touched since the first night of the Blitz which, if you remember, was 1940. So, for over fifteen years, it had remained in the same condition. It was leaning over to one side, and the top windows were boarded up, as well as half of the ones below. One of the top windows had a gap in it, which had encouraged, it seemed, the entire pigeon population of the East End to roost in the attic and top floor. When it came to the signage, the gold leaf lettering spelling out our name was barely legible through rain damage. It was in a shocking state ... something had to be done.

This is no way to run a business, I thought. No wonder people aren't coming in; they probably think we've closed up. Even though I was out there nearly every day, polishing the front step and cleaning what was left of the windows and scrubbing the floorboards inside, until they were bleached white, it was, as the saying goes, 'trying to make a silk purse out of a sow's ear', and I'd had enough.

Taking a deep breath, I walked inside. Uncle was sitting as usual, by the desk reading the newspaper and enjoying his early morning cup of tea and a Woodbine.

'What are we going to do about this shop? We can't go on like this,' I said, as forcefully as I could.

'Blimey! Who's rattled your cage? Bursting in here all stroppy ... what's brought this on, had a row with Joan?' he asked, looking at me, while at the same time annoyingly licking his finger to turn the pages of the paper.

'No, I haven't had a row with Joan. Have you looked at the state of this shop? It's a health hazard. The thing's going to fall in on us soon.'

'Of course I've looked at the sodding shop. I sit here all day. What d'you think I'm looking at? There's no way I can afford to do any work. We've barely got enough money to survive, and I haven't heard the council banging on the door offering to help – they're happy enough to take the rent every week though, aren't they? I resigned myself a long time ago to the fact that if the place falls down, it falls down ... nothing I can do about it, boy,' he said calmly.

'Oh, charming!' I said. 'But we *can't* leave it like this ... it's ridiculous!' I was starting to get worked up at his casual attitude. 'I'm going to ring the council to see what they can do.'

He laughed. Well, good luck there. After the last fiasco at Lansdowne Road, I won't hold my breath.'

Several years beforehand our garages and stables in Lansdowne Road had been taken off us by the council, under a compulsory purchase order. Tom was completely devastated by this, as his father had purchased the land back in 1881, when he started out in the business, and it should've been worth a lot of money, but he ended up getting virtually nothing for it. This had made him very bitter and suspicious of anything involving the council.

'We've no alternative,' I said. 'So I might as well ring them, what've we got to lose?'

That afternoon I spoke to a Mr Fletcher from West Ham Council. I announced who I was, and where I was calling from, and told him I'd like to discuss the situation regarding our premises.

'Good afternoon, Mr Cribb, yes, of course – if you just give me a moment I'll retrieve your file,' he said. A few minutes later he came back on the line. 'Sorry, but I have no record of you.'

'No record?' I replied. 'But there must be!'

'No, definitely not. I've checked the files and there's nothing there,' he explained.

'Well, for the last thirty years we've been paying rent every Friday to a man on a bike called Eric, so I don't know where that's been going,' I said angrily.

'Oh?' he said. 'How very odd. I'll look into it some more and I'll get back to you, if I may. But before I go, could you explain to me what the actual enquiry is concerning?'

'Yes, of course. The premises were badly damaged during the Blitz. In fact, we were the only shop left standing after that first night of bombings and we carried on throughout the entire war with a half-bombed shop. It's crooked, the top windows are boarded up, as well as half of the bottom ones, and we'd like the council to carry out repairs for us, as we can't continue working under these conditions,' I explained.

I could hear him scribbling away at the other end. 'Right you are, then, got every-thing I need. I'll contact you by letter in the next week or so. Goodbye.' He then hung up.

Not registered. How could that be? We'd been paying rent for so many years to this man Eric, so where had it been going? Per-haps he was pretending to be from the council and just pocketing the money – stranger things have happened. But thinking about it afterwards, I thought it odd that we'd never had a rent increase. I couldn't tell you how long we'd been paying £1.10s a week, but it was for as long as I could remember. Maybe I had stirred up a hornets' nest and things would become a whole lot worse.

I told Uncle that I'd spoken to them but not the details of the conversation – only that they would look into it and write back shortly.

'Can't wait!' he said sarcastically.

It was about two weeks later when the letter dropped on the mat. I quickly tore it open. It read in bold letters: 'Notice to Quit'. We had to vacate the premises by 1 September – six months away. Heaven help me, what had I done?

'I told you not to start making yourself busy, didn't I?' Uncle shouted across the shop. 'You just can't resist it, can you, poking your nose in? I knew no good would come out of it. Now what are we supposed to do?'

'I don't know,' I said, my voice echoing vacantly around the room. I was devastated.

'No, of course you don't know, that's always been your sodding trouble.' I called Mr Fletcher several times but all he said was, 'Sorry, Mr Cribb, out of my hands now – nothing I can do about it, I'm afraid.'

What was the point? It was all over.

A couple of months went by, and I'd started to feel very down. Uncle was down too but we had no choice but to carry on until the last. I was polishing a coffin in the front window one day when the door opened and in walked a young man.

He was dressed very fashionably; his ginger hair was slicked back with a quiff at the front; he had drainpipe trousers and winkle-picker shoes, a jacket with leather patches on the elbows, a white shirt and a 'slim Jim' tie.

'Good morning,' he said, smiling broadly. 'Are you Mr Thomas Cribb?'

'No, that's my uncle. He's out the back. I'll go and fetch him for you. Who should I say is calling?'

'Mr Anchor. I'm the Junior Architect from Stratford Council,' he explained.

The council ... what on earth was this about?

I walked out to the office. 'Chap here from the council to see you.'

'Oh, for the love of God, what's he want? Probably wants to chuck us out even earlier!'

'I don't think so. He's a junior architect,' I explained.

'A *junior* architect ... see! Whatever he's here for the buggers wouldn't even send us a proper grown-up one. Did you ask him what he wants?' he asked, puzzled.

'No, you'd better come out and see him.'

We both walked outside. Uncle shook his hand and looked him up and down. He then turned away, pulling me with him. 'Excuse me a moment,' he said, looking over his shoulder at him. He then whispered in my ear: 'I'm not dealing with this scruffy bastard; you'll have to do it.' And with that he walked back to the office and shut the door behind him.

Personally, I thought he looked very smart, but to Uncle, anyone who wasn't wearing a bowler hat would've been classified as scruffy.

'Sorry, Mr Anchor, my uncle's not feeling too well, maybe I can help you?' I said, as I walked back, pointing to a seat by the desk.

Out of his bag he pulled a large sketch pad and pen. 'Right now I'd like, if you can, for you to describe to me in detail what your ideal premises would require?'

'My ideal premises?' I asked, dumbfounded.

'Yes, what an undertakers would require to bring them up to the modern standards of today.'

'I'm sorry to sound so stupid, but what are you actually here for? Is it a survey or something?'

He leant forward and clasped his hands together on top of the desk, looking at me, still smiling.

'Survey? Goodness, no! I'm here to find out *exactly* what you'd want your new premises to be like. I've been instructed to draw up plans for the new shop, which is to be built just along the road here at 112

Rathbone Street.'

'New shop? The last letter I had from the council was two months ago, and it was giving us notice to quit by September. We've heard absolutely nothing since,' I said, amazed.

'How odd! But I can assure you that your new premises have been passed by the council to be built here. All you need to do is tell me what you want.'

'Just a minute, let me go in and explain what you've just told me to my uncle. I'm sure he'll have something to say,' I said, hurrying back to the office.

'Of course, take your time,' he said, lounging back in his chair.

I closed the office door behind me and quietly repeated to Tom what had been said.

'New premises? They're winding us up, that's what they're doing!' he shouted.

'Shh! Why on earth would they do that?' I whispered.

'How the sodding hell would I know,' he replied. 'And don't you dare tell me to shush, boy!'

'Look, I'm sorry. I just don't want him to hear us arguing. Why don't you just come out and listen to what he's got to say.' I was so frustrated.

'I AM NOT GOING TO WASTE MY TIME SITTING WITH THAT LITTLE TWIT! Now clear off. You sodding started it, you get on with it!'

I never did get around to telling you that his nickname was 'Tom Sod-em-all', did I?

I walked out, shutting the door behind me. I now felt embarrassed that we'd been overheard, but the fact that he'd been called a 'twit' seemed to have gone unnoticed, as he was obviously deep in thought, drawing on his pad.

I heard the office door creak open. I glanced around, thinking he had changed his mind, but all he'd done was open it so he could sit and listen to what we were saying.

I sat there for several hours going over exactly what we would want. A Chapel of Rest was definitely going to be top of the list. I couldn't believe it. I was like a child in a sweet shop. I occasionally glanced around at the office and could see Uncle leaning back in his chair, his ear close to the gap, with a Woodbine clasped between his fingers.

'Well, I think I have everything I need,' said Mr Anchor. 'I'll be in touch.' I saw him out and then sat back down in a state of shock. Uncle walked back in and we looked at one another.

'Well, would you believe it?' I said, laughing.

'No, I don't, and I won't believe it until it's built and we're sitting in it!' he said.

Around three weeks later I took a phone call. 'Mr Cribb, it's Mr Anchor here, hope you're keeping well. I just wanted to ask you if you wouldn't mind popping into the Stratford office when it's convenient, as I would like to show you something.'

'Of course, I'll be happy too. How about tomorrow?'

I arrived at the offices as arranged. I was on my own. Uncle, still not having any of it, decided to stay put. I was shown into his office and there, on the table, was a model of our new shop. It was amazing. Everything was exactly as I had requested it should be. He'd done a wonderful job.

'That looks fantastic,' I said, still staring at the model. I couldn't take my eyes off it.

'Good, glad you like it. It's already been passed by the board, so all we have to do now is get it built,' he said understatedly.

I left those offices in a complete trance. Built? They were going to start building? We still hadn't received one letter from the council about this – absolutely nothing. It was absurd, all this going on without one word of correspondence. I could appreciate why Uncle was so apprehensive about it all.

I returned to the shop in a state of excitement.

'Have you been drinking?' he asked, eyeing me suspiciously. 'This whole thing stinks, Stan. There's something fishy going on and I don't like it one bit. This type of thing just doesn't happen ... they can't be doing it for nothing, can they? They'll want something and we haven't got anything, so what's going to happen once the thing's built – if it gets that far, mind you!'

I could understand why he felt suspicious. I had my own reservations, so I decided to ring the council again.

'Hello, Mr Fletcher. Mr Cribb again from Cribb's undertakers,' I explained.

'Oh yes, good afternoon. What can I do for you?' he asked.

'Well, I've just come from Stratford Council and they've shown me a model of the new premises, which is to be built in the very near future, but we're extremely concerned about the finances of this property. I wanted to tell you that we've no money to pay for them, if that's what you're expecting. You see, we don't want to reach the point of the building being finished and then discover you're invoicing us for the works. We'd rather lay our cards on the table now before it gets that far. After all, the only form of communication we've had was back in March, which was the notice to quit,' I said.

'Ah yes, I see what you mean, much better to get these things sorted beforehand, quite agree. Hang on, let me get your file out.' I then waited a few minutes. 'Right, now let's see, you said you were paying rent on your other property, so it seems sensible to carry on the same way with this one, don't you think? So, how much would you be willing to pay?' he asked.

Once again I was taken aback. 'How much am I willing to pay? I've got no idea!' I said.

'Have you got a figure in mind?'

'Um, interesting question ... now let me think.' I could hear his fingers strumming on the desk. 'How about we say £600 per year with a twenty-one-year lease – does that sound alright with you?'

I paused for a second. I couldn't believe my ears! 'That sounds acceptable,' I blurted out. I didn't know what else to say. I was in a state of shock.

'Marvellous! Problem solved then. Well, that was easy, wasn't it! It's been very nice doing business with you, Mrs Cribb. I bid you farewell.' And with that he hung up the phone.

Mrs Cribb? He'd called me Mrs Cribb! Now, I was alright up until that point. I mean, was it just a slip of the tongue or was the man genuinely round the twist? I was so confused by everything that had been going on for the last four months that I'd started to analyse every little detail, trying to justify what on earth was going on around me. The only conclusion I had was that some form of madness had taken hold.

The building work started around the end of 1958. Every day I would stand outside the shop, watching it go up. It was a sight for sore eyes. Towards the end, as the windows starting going in, with T. CRIBB & Sons etched into them, it felt that it was actually happening for real.

Eight months later it was finished. We locked up the old premises, which the council had allowed us to stay in until the new one was built, thank goodness, and moved virtually next door into the new place. It was one of the best days of my life.

As we sat down for the first time to have a cup of tea, I turned to Uncle and said, 'Well, do you believe it now?'

'It's absolutely perfect, boy. But I still don't believe we aren't going to be paying for it. Somebody will want a back-hander one day, you mark my words. I'm never going to have any peace because every time the postman delivers a letter I'll think it's a bill from the council.'

True to his word, for the next thirteen years every time an official-looking envelope dropped through our letterbox he thought the 'day of reckoning' had come, but it didn't; and we never received a bill.

14

Nell Vale and Mrs Pryce's Son
1961 (age 33)

Since the opening of the new premises, the
business took off again, thank heavens. I was
regularly getting night calls a couple of
times a week. I was losing out on my beauty
sleep, but it was worth it. We couldn't have
been happier with the way the new premises
had taken off.

As a result of these late night calls, the
curiosity of my two sons – Graham (who by
then was nine, and John, six) had been
ignited. It must have been very mysterious
for them to hear their dad talking on the
phone in the dead of night and then seeing
him head off into the dark.

They would stand on the hall landing in
their pyjamas listening to my conversations
and, in the morning over breakfast, I would
feel as if I was under interrogation from the
'East End Inquisition', as they'd want to
know, as my grandma always said, 'the ins
and outs of a cat's arse'.

I vividly remember one week I had two
call-outs that would remain etched into my

memory for ever, as they were both so out of the ordinary. The first came at around 2.30 a.m.

'Good morning, Cribb and Son,' I said, in as clear a voice as I could muster.

'Mr Cribb, is that you?' A woman's voice came from the other end. 'My name's Nell Vale and my husband died about an hour ago and I ... I don't know what to do. Can you help me please?' She then began to cry.

'Yes, of course, Mrs Vale. I'm so sorry for your loss. You're obviously very upset. What would you like me to do?' I asked. When we had calls at this time of the morning from the general public there were several things they might ask us to do. Either go round and collect the body immediately, or, if they had members of the family all together, they may ask us round to discuss what their next move would be and arrangements would be made to go back and collect the body in the morning. Every circumstance was different and, depending on the emotional state of the person calling, I would not normally ask them what they wanted me to do, but wait for them to tell me and then work around that – but this lady seemed confused.

'Could you come round? I know it's late but, it's just...' The crying continued.

'Of course, it's not a problem, what's your address?'

'I'm in Montpelier Gardens, East Ham,'

she sobbed.

'I'll be there in around half an hour, is that OK?'

'Yes, thank you, Mr Cribb. I'll see you shortly.' And with that she hung up.

As I went to walk back upstairs, there, with their faces flushed and hands clamped around the banisters, were the boys, looking like a couple of miniature convicts. My daughter Susan, who was just a toddler, was happily tucked up in her cot.

'Where you going Dad?' Graham shouted. I don't know why but he could never speak in normal tones. He had a voice like a 'town bull'. I'd often tried to get him to lower his voice to a bellow but alas to no avail.

'Shush, you'll wake your mum and sister; get back to bed *now*,' I said quietly.

'But Dad, I want to know where you're going?' he insisted.

'I'm not going to tell you again. Go to bed! I'll tell you all about it in the morning,' I said impatiently.

Not one for ever taking 'no' for an answer, he piped up: 'Can I come with you?'

God, give me strength! He was a nightmare. Hardly a day went by when I wondered whose genes he'd inherited. He'd try the patience of a saint.

I stood glaring at him through the banister, and it's funny what one particular look can achieve. I'd perfected it with him over the years, and, thinking about it, I must have inherited it from my mum and I found it worked far more effectively than words. He was back in bed within seconds, with John right behind him. He'd learnt during his few years on earth that when his elder brother spoke it was always wise to keep out of it, as it inevitably led to trouble.

It never ceased to amaze me how two sons from the same parents could be so unalike. There was unquestionably nothing remotely similar about them, either in looks or personality. Graham, tall, thick-set with fair hair who, if based on a comic character, would be the more aggravating brother of 'Dennis the Menace', whereas John, slight build and very dark, was to be honest, the actual son my mother would have loved: 'Little Lord Fauntleroy'. They drove each other mad – and still do – but not as much as they did when they were kids.

John was always extremely tidy: clothes hung up and neatly put away, very studious, quiet and home-loving whereas Graham: untidy, clothes permanently on the floor, hated school, extremely noisy and always wanted to be out – more commonly known as 'a bloody nuisance'. As soon as he was old enough to move out and could do what he wanted, when he wanted, we got along just fine.

Years later, when he initially wanted to

join the business, I was taken aback, as I always thought his true vocation was at sea. He would've made a marvellous stand-in foghorn if the ships broke down, but no, he wanted to join us, as did John.

Susan, on the other hand, was a normal, well-adjusted girl who didn't cause us any problems, and growing up didn't show a lot of interest in joining the firm, but she obviously enjoyed being part of an undertaking family, as she ended up marrying one.

After making sure the boys were back in bed, I went into the bedroom, got changed and headed off. These night-time call-outs normally meant I was away for roughly an hour and a half.

It was approaching 3 a.m. as I pulled up outside the house. I knocked on the door and waited. When there wasn't an answer I knocked again, harder. I then heard a 'rat-tat'. I stepped back, looked around, and heard it again, coming from above. I saw Mrs Vale at the bedroom window mouthing, 'I won't be a minute.'

I put my thumb up; she was obviously with her husband – maybe preparing him for us. A few minutes later the door was opened by an extremely large lady who was very tearful and out of breath. Funnily enough, you didn't see people that large in those days, but if you did they'd generally be described as 'on the plump side', 'stout', as my grandma would say, or 'having something wrong with her glands', but this lady was well past those adjectives – she was a right whopper!

Her hair was tied up in a headscarf, and poking out from underneath I could see metal 'wave grips' clamped onto her hair instead of the more popular rollers. (How women ever got any sleep wearing these contraptions I'll never know.) She still had her slippers on and her housecoat could've comfortably doubled up to give a troop of scouts adequate shelter for an adventure weekend. Obviously her husband's death had happened suddenly and she hadn't time to change.

'Oh, I'm sorry I took so long to answer the floor, Mr Cribb, please come in, go through to the back room,' she said, pointing down the hall. As she joined me in the living room I held out my hand and she shook it gently, smiling. 'Pleasure to meet you, Mrs Vale,' I said.

'Thank you for coming at such short notice, and I'm sorry,' she said, touching her 'grips' and looking down at her nightwear. 'I'm not properly dressed but everything's happened so quickly. I just didn't know what to do. I've never had to do this type of thing before, and I'm sorry I couldn't take you into the front room, but the fire's not made up and as it's so cold its best if we sit in here where it's nice and warm. Please make yourself at home. Would you like a nice cup of tea?'

'That would be lovely, thank you,' I said, thinking it would give her time to compose herself. She seemed better than she had been on the phone, but I didn't want to rush her. I've learnt over the years that collecting a body and organising funerals are not simple tasks; a lot of psychology goes into it. When you initially see someone they may talk about anything except what you're actually there for. I understand how painful it is and I let them talk as much as they liked until they feel ready to get down to the task at hand. If she did want me to take the body away tonight, I would have to contact Jack, who would then cycle to the workshop, pick up the van and a 'shell' and meet me here. That would take around an hour, but until I had sat her down to see exactly what she had in mind, everything was on hold. I'd assumed the doctor had already been and gone and left the death certificate but, to be honest, I didn't have a clue what had been done, and I was secretly hoping that Mr Vale wasn't as large as his wife. If that was the case then a 'bespoke' shell would have to be made to fit him, and it would take more than two of us to move him. I had to get some information soon.

I could see there were lots of photos

around the room, so I got up to take a look. As I was looking at one in particular Mrs Vale returned. 'That's George, my husband,' she said, as she bustled in carrying the tray with a pot of tea and a plate of homemade cake. 'He breeds canaries.' She paused, put down the tray, took her handkerchief from her pocket and wiped her eyes. 'I have to say *bred* canaries now, don't I?' she said, blowing her nose.

Well, at least one problem was answered straight away. Mr Vale stood proudly holding onto a cage in which sat a beautiful canary. As you find in many couples, 'opposites attract' and this saying certainly applied here. He was in fact extraordinarily slight and delicate, so much that I could've probably carried him out myself. In fact, it looked as if even holding up the birdcage was an effort for him.

'Sit down, Mrs Vale – here let me pour the tea,' I said, as we both sat in adjoining armchairs with the table in between.

'He bred the best canaries in the country. People used to come from all over the place to buy them from him for breeding ... it was his passion. Please help yourself to a nice piece of cake. I only made it this morning,' she said, taking a slice for herself.

'I love birds too,' I said, wiping the crumbs from my mouth. 'I keep chickens but one day I hope to have an aviary and keep exotic birds. How many canaries did Mr Vale have?'

'Oh, now let's see, he must have at least eighty and when the dawn breaks – to hear them singing! It's so beautiful. It lifts the spirits. Shall I take you to see them after we've finished our tea?' she asked eagerly.

'I'd love that, but it's so dark we won't see much,' I said.

'Oh, don't you worry about that. It's got all the mod cons up there, Mr Cribb. He put in electric light and everything. I think he thought more of those birds than he did his own child,' she said with a wry smile.

After I'd been sitting there nearly an hour listening to her stories, she seemed to be a lot more composed, so I thought the time was right to broach the subject of removing Mr Vale from the house, as time was marching on.

'So ... it was sudden, I take it? It's always such a shock when–'

'Well, no, it wasn't sudden as in unexpected. He'd been ill for a number of years. He had emphysema, you see. He'd been a very heavy smoker all his life. In the latter years he wasn't able to go to the bird shows like he used to as he was constantly fighting for his breath. A few weeks ago he got a bad dose of the flu, which went straight to his chest. The doctor put on his death certificate that death was caused by emphysema and pneumonia, but even though it wasn't sudden-sudden, if you know what I mean, it's still a huge shock.' She then pulled her handkerchief out and started crying again.

I now knew the doctor had been in and certified death, so another question was out of the way. 'Of course it is. These times are the hardest we have to face,' I said, leaning forward and topping up her teacup.

'Oh, that's gone cold now. Let me go and make a nice fresh one; nothing worse than coddly tea,' she said, sniffing and wiping her nose, but she managed a brief smile as she stood up.

'I'm fine, no more tea for me, thank you. In fact I should be making a move soon. I've a very early start in the morning and I've been here over an hour already,' I said, making to stand up.

'But you haven't been down to the aviary yet. You said you *loved* birds,' she said sadly.

'I do, it's just with it being dark outside I don't think it'll do them any good if we go in there and turn the lights on. They'll be all puffed up and asleep. We don't want to shock them, do we? I promise I'll see them next time I'm around, in the daylight,' I explained, hoping that she wouldn't insist. I was shattered, I'd only had two hours' sleep before coming to see her and we had a ten o'clock funeral.

'Well, if you don't think it's a good idea let

me show you this, just quickly before you go.' She went over to the sideboard and pulled out one of the biggest photo albums I've seen. I suddenly felt slightly hysterical. This album would take hours to go through and I just couldn't do it. I *had* to think quickly. 'Have you a toilet I can use please? Tea always has that effect on me,' I said quickly.

'Yes, of course, it's still out the back, I'm afraid. The birds got all the mod-cons, not us.' She smiled again. 'Just round to your right, there's a light inside.'

I went and sat on the toilet seat. I had to get out *now*. If I started looking at that album I'd be stuck for another hour at least, and she obviously didn't want to discuss the removal of her husband. I might as well go home and sort it out in the morning. I rested my head against the cold wall, preparing myself for when I went back in.

'Mr Cribb, Mr Cribb, are you OK?' A shout accompanied by violent banging woke me with a start. I was completely disorientated.

'Mr Cribb, can you hear me?' a panicky voice came from outside.

Realisation dawned. 'Yes, yes, I'm fine,' I said, still not with it.

'Are you sure? I thought you might've come over bad or something,' she said, concerned.

I opened the door. I was so embarrassed. 'I'm sorry, I must have fallen asleep.'

'Oh, thank goodness for that! She laughed

from the relief of knowing that she didn't have two bodies on her hands in one evening. 'You poor thing, you must be exhausted to fall asleep in an outside lav,' she chuckled. 'Come on, come back in the warm; it's parky out here,' she said, rubbing her hands together.

I was like an imbecile as I followed her into the warm scullery. 'Now you sit back down and pull yourself together; you're all groggy. I'll go and make you a cup of strong coffee to wake you up.'

'No, thank you. I *really* must go,' I insisted.

'But you can't drive home like that! You'll fall asleep at the wheel and I don't want that on my conscience. Come on, now, sit yourself down,' she said, virtually pushing me back into the armchair. I was powerless to resist. It felt like a freight train forcing me back. She then picked the photo album up and put it on my lap. 'There you go, that'll take your mind off sleep. Have a good look through that,' she said excitedly as she bustled back to the scullery. I had a sneaky suspicion she would've put a little skip into her step if her weight had allowed.

I looked at the front cover. It read: 'Bird shows – 1960–1964'. Another bout of panic hit me. We were now in 1968. I quickly turned around and looked at the slightly open door of the sideboard and spotted another album of a similar size.

254

I felt weepy. I was trapped.

I started mechanically going through it when she returned with the coffee. 'What do you think, Mr Cribb, lovely aren't they?'

'Yes, they're beautiful. He was obviously a very gifted breeder. You must have been very proud,' I said wearily.

'Oh, I was ... *so* proud of him.' She then decided to manoeuvre herself onto the arm of my chair, pinning me in as if she was intentionally reducing my chances of escape. She took off her glasses, breathed on them, then started polishing them with alacrity on the corner of her housecoat. 'Right!' she said. 'I'm ready. Now let's turn back to the beginning and I'll explain each photo to you,' she said gleefully.

I mechanically turned page after page. Her huge body so close to mine was radiating so much heat it felt like a huge hot-water bottle. My eyes were getting heavier and heavier, and her enormous bosom, which was pushing against my shoulder, felt like a lovely soft pillow and I longed to lay my head against it and drift off; how I didn't I don't know. As we came to the end, a wave of relief flooded through me. I could see by my watch it was close to 5.45 a.m.

'Lovely!' I said, quickly closing the album and placing it on the table. 'And I look forward to seeing the real thing when I come back next time.' I started to dislodge myself in order to stand up but thought better of it as she was still perched on the arm and if I got up suddenly the counter-balance would be lost and I'd send her flying.

'But what am I going to do with them, Mr Cribb?' she said. 'Our son isn't interested. I'm obviously going to have to get rid of them, but I don't know where or...' She trailed off, deep in thought and started to wipe her eyes again.

'Just take each day as it comes, Mrs Vale. There's no rush to do anything. It'll all fall into place, just give yourself time. Now, I'm sorry, but I *must* be going.'

'Oh listen!' she said, putting her hand on my shoulder, pushing me further down into the armchair. She cocked her head to the window. 'Can you hear it?'

'What?' I asked, not particularly bothered.

'The birds!'

Oh, please God, NO!

'They've woken up, they've started to sing. Dawn's here already,' she said excitedly, standing up. 'We can go up to see them now.' As she stood up I shot up at the same time, so quickly black spots appeared in front of my gritty eyes.

'No!' I said, louder than I should've done. I put my hand onto the mantelpiece as a wave of lightheadedness swept over me. I couldn't spend another hour there. 'I *have* to go,' I said pitifully. She looked surprised at my unexpected outburst. 'I'm sorry I raised my voice ... it's just that I do need to get back, as I said I have a very early funeral.'

I then heard a key in the front door. She quickly turned to the clock. 'Goodness, it's our son John. I didn't expect him so soon,' she said, as she headed over to the hall door, calling, 'I'm in here, John, you've made good time. I didn't expect you for another hour or so.'

A man in his late thirties walked in carrying a small suitcase, and he looked puzzled when he saw me standing there.

'Mr Cribb, this is John, my son, he's come to help with the arrangements. John, this is Mr Cribb the undertaker, he's been here nearly all night keeping me company.'

'Pleased to meet you, Mr Cribb,' he said, shaking my hand. 'Thank you for sitting with Mum.'

'No problem at all,' I smiled, relieved that I could now leave. Turning back to his mother I said, 'Would you mind if I popped upstairs before I go?'

She looked at me oddly. 'You want to go upstairs?'

'Yes, if that's OK, just to take a quick look.'

'Well, OK, do you want me to come with you?' she asked.

'No, no that's fine; I'll just be a few minutes.'

I walked into the hallway and she was

behind me. 'The room at the top is our spare room, the one along the passage was John's, and the one at the front is ours.'

'OK, thank you, I shan't be a minute.' I went up, taking the stairs two at a time I only had to measure him and I could be on my way.

I headed directly to the room at the front, but as I looked towards the bed it was empty. What on earth ... where the hell was he? I was even tempted to drop to my knees and look under the bed, but even in my sleep-deprived state knew I was being ridiculous. I headed back to John's old room ... nothing, then the spare room – nothing!

'Are you looking for something, Mr Cribb?' Mrs Vale called from the bottom of the stairs.

'Where's your husband?' I asked, utterly confused.

'In the hospital,' she said strangely.

'In the hospital!' I said, as I started to walk downstairs. 'But I thought he'd died here.'

'What on earth gave you that idea?' she said surprised.

I was furious, but I couldn't let on.

'Well, normally when we get a night call it's to collect the body or make arrangements to pick them up early in the morning. I've never had a call-out at that time of the morning when there hasn't been a body,' I said, as calmly as I could.

Just then, John came to the doorway. 'I thought it was odd you were here, Mr Cribb. That's why I was a bit taken aback when I saw you.' He turned to his mother. 'Mum, I can't *believe* you called out the undertakers. Why did you do it?'

The poor woman looked mortified. 'Oh God, I feel so embarrassed, it's just ... well, I didn't know what to do.' She looked at John. 'I knew you would take at least four hours to get here after I called, and I knew I wouldn't be able to sleep.' She then turned to me. 'Your advert says call us night or day. I told you I hadn't done this before. I just thought, well, I just thought you'd come and keep me company until John arrived. Oh dear. I feel *such* a fool,' she cried.

'I'm so sorry,' John said, as he glanced over at his mum who had now collapsed with humiliation into the nearest armchair. 'I can only apologise.'

'Please don't,' I said through gritted teeth. 'It's been a first for me, but as long as your mum's OK and I've helped her get through the night, then that's what's important.'

'Thank you, I appreciate it. I'll take Mum to get all the paperwork done and then I'll bring her down to Rathbone Street to make the funeral arrangements,' he said.

'Fine, I'll see you both later. See you later, Mrs Vale,' I said, looking back to the armchair.

'Cheerio, Mr Cribb, and I'm *so* sorry for...'

'No problem, forget about it,' I said quickly, in case she started again. I shook hands with the son and finally headed home.

But I still couldn't believe it. All night I'd sat there thinking there was a body upstairs and all the time he was in the hospital mortuary. I'd never experienced anything like it. I didn't particular like night-time call-outs. I did them because I had to, but most of the time I was on autopilot and just got on with it ... but this!

When I got home I only had time for a quick wash, changed into my suit and headed off to the shop. Luckily the boys weren't up, so I didn't have to deal with a barrage of questions from the 'inquisition' – that could wait until later and, by then, hopefully they would have forgotten all about it.

Uncle was already sitting there with Jack, going over the morning's funeral arrangements with their cups of tea.

'Dear God, you look awful!' he said helpfully, as I hung my coat up.

'Thanks,' I said feebly.

'What you been doing all night? Was one of the children playing up?' he asked.

'No, nothing as simple as that. At least I would've got some sleep, as Joan would've dealt with it. But listen to this. I had a call-out at 2.30 a.m. thinking there was a body to collect from a house and all along the chap had died in hospital. Do you believe it? The lady just wanted me there for company until her son arrived from Oxford. Over three hours I was there!' I said angrily.

'Well?' he said.

'What do you mean, "Well?"?' I asked in disbelief.

'Well, what's wrong with that? What happened that's upset you so much?'

'I got there at three, she was a bit upset and I didn't want to bring up removing her husband before I'd settled her down. She asked me if I wanted a cup of tea which I said "yes" to in order to give her a bit more time,' I explained.

'That was nice of her; especially at that time of the morning don't you think that was nice, Jack?'

'Very nice, Tom,' he exclaimed, nodding.

'Then?' he said, picking up his cup.

'Then she told me how her husband bred canaries...'

'Really? Now *that's* interesting ... were they good ones?' he asked, picking up a biscuit and dunking it in his tea.

'Yes, lovely; he won Best in Show loads of times.'

'No! That's marvellous and you love birds ... so why weren't you interested?' he said curiously.

'It's not that I wasn't interested,' I said angrily. 'I was *shattered* and knew we had an early start and wanted to get some sleep. I needed to find out if she wanted us to take her husband away but I couldn't get her to talk about it and thought I was wasting my time.'

'Wasting your time! Comforting a woman who's just lost her husband, who seems to me was being very nice to you and all you could think of was sleeping – that's a disgrace, boy. What d'you think, Jack?' he asked.

'Disgraceful,' he said, tutting and shaking his head.

'But she was purposefully keeping me there,' I said. 'I even fell asleep in her toilet...'

'WHAT!' he said, leaning back in the chair and holding his head. 'You fell asleep in her sodding toilet. I don't believe it!'

'I went out there to think and just fell asleep. She found me twenty minutes later, thought I'd come over bad, so took me back in and insisted I have a strong coffee, as she wouldn't let me drive home in case I had an accident.'

'This woman sounds a saint. What time was it now?'

'Nearly 4.30,' I said quietly. Jack was sitting looking at me with his mouth hanging open still shaking his head.

'So you had the coffee and left...'

'No, *that's* the point, she made me the coffee then gave me an enormous photo album full of her husband's achievements *and* she was big! I've never seen a woman, or man for that matter, *so* big. She then decided to sit on the arm of my chair, pinning me in and looking right over my shoulder she went through it page by page, which took another hour ... I was literally trapped. If I'd got up she would've gone flying! *Then* just as we'd finished she says "Listen" and looks towards the window,' I said, my voice becoming a bit pitiful.

Uncle leans forward. 'What was you listening for?' he says eagerly.

'The canaries had woken up and had starting singing,' I explained.

'Oh lovely! I love hearing a canary sing, don't you, Jack, lifts the spirits.'

'It certainly does,' he said and nodded again.

These two were like a double act; I was starting to get worked up again.

'Then?' Uncle said.

'She only wanted to take me down to see them!'

'Now don't tell me you didn't go,' he said, leaning back again.

'NO, I DIDN'T! I told her I couldn't, I had to go it was late, I would see them next time.' I was exasperated.

Well, that seems *very* rude to me, boy ... very rude ... what'd you think, Jack?' he asked.

'Very rude,' he said, now shaking his head.

I jumped up, grabbing my coat. 'RIGHT! I've had enough of this ... you two are unbelievable! I'm going up the yard to check on everything,' I said.

'Hold your horses, boy!' Uncle shouted. 'You haven't finished your story ... so what happened then?'

'What happened then? I'll tell you what happened then! Her son turns up from Oxford, who she's been waiting for all night, and *that's* when I found out the reason why I was there. I shot upstairs to take some quick measurements before I left only to find Mr Vale wasn't there. He was, as Mrs Vale then decides to tell me, in the bloody hospital mortuary,' I screamed frustratedly.

His mouth started to twitch.

I was still holding my coat, so I turned around, opened the door and headed out. I was too tired to deal with this. As I put my hand in my pocket to get out the car keys I realised I'd left them on the desk. I turned back. As I reached the door I stopped and looked inside, and there they were, Uncle Tom leaning against the wall with his arms wrapped around his middle and Jack laid out across the desk both in hernia-producing convulsions. When I opened the door and walked back in they looked up quickly with straight faces, thinking a customer had walked in but when they saw it was me, collapsed again. I grabbed the keys, slammed the door behind me and headed off to the workshop. As I drove along a smile did creep onto my lips. If only I hadn't been so exhausted or if the story had been about someone else I would have found it highly amusing too.

Mrs Vale and her son arrived in the shop later that afternoon. She walked in looking extremely sheepish, carrying a lovely Victoria sponge.

'This is for you, Mr Cribb. I can't apologise enough...' she started to say.

'*Please,* no more apologies, Mrs Vale. Now sit down and let me reciprocate your kindness. I'll make you a nice cup of tea and we can share your lovely cake and sort out all the arrangements.'

She smiled shyly.

After Mr Vale's funeral I made a point of going round every Sunday to help her clean out the birds. I don't know why; I just felt a bit sorry that she was on her own and she had all those birds to look after. I even gave her a hand phoning customers from her husband's contacts who had purchased birds from him in the past, to see if they would like to buy some more. It took a month or so, but in the end we managed to find good homes for all of them except one. He was her husband's favourite, and given pride of place in the living room by the window. He was lovingly named Georgie, and every morning, without fail, he filled her little house with birdsong.

A few days later the ringing of the phone filled our quiet house. As usual I ran downstairs to answer it.

'Mr Cribb, it's the police. An intruder's been caught trying to get into your shop. A passing driver saw him and alerted us. Fortunately we got there before he broke in,' the, officer explained.

'What a bloody nuisance!' I said angrily.

'I agree. I'm sorry to have woken you but obviously we had to inform you what had happened,' the officer said. 'But there's no need for you to go down there, as he didn't gain entry, but obviously it's entirely up to you if you want to check everything. They're taking him back to the station now to charge him with attempted burglary. It's all a bit sad though – apparently all he keeps going on about is wanting to see his mum.'

'What! D'you know anything else?' I asked.

'No, that's all the information I've got.'

'Look, it'll take me fifteen minutes to get down there. D'you think the police could wait for me and maybe we can get this sorted out?' I asked.

'I don't know. Hang on, I'll have a quick word.'

After a brief while the voice returned. 'The

officers said they'll wait for you, as he's still going on about seeing her,' he explained.

'OK, I'm on my way, thank you,' I said.

Luckily enough the boys were out like lights that night, so I was saved from an interrogation. I quickly got changed and headed off. The police were parked outside. As I pulled up one of them explained to me again what had happened. Apparently they'd had a call around 1.45 a.m. that a man was seen trying to get in through the front door. By the time they'd arrived he'd given up on the door and had started to scale the back wall.

'I heard that he keeps on about wanting to see his mum?' I said.

'That's right. Said she died last week and the funeral's tomorrow and that he wants to see her. He's been drinking but he's not drunk.'

'Would you mind bringing him over so I can have a word.'

'I'll get him,' he said, walking back to the car.

He then fetched over a small, skinny, bedraggled-looking chap in his late thirties. He looked wild, shifty, his eyes kept darting around as if he thought somebody was after him, and he had a horrible habit of continually sniffing and wiping his nose onto the back of his hand.

'You want to see your mum, I hear. What's

her name?' I asked.

'Margaret Pryce. She died last week. I've been away, 'aven't seen 'er for years. I want to see 'er!' he said angrily.

'Well, why don't you come back early in the morning and–'

'NO! I *told* ya, I want to see 'er *now*. I've *got* to see 'er!'He was very agitated.

The policeman looked at me, raising his eyebrows. 'Come on, lad,' he said, taking his arm. 'You're out of order getting stroppy with this gentleman. He's got out of his bed to try and sort you out. Let's get you back to the station; you can have some coffee, pull yourself together and...'

He yanked his arm from the policeman's grip, shouting that he had to see his mother. He was glaring at me.

I didn't like him one bit.

His arm was then pulled up behind his back, causing him to scream in pain. 'That's it! Come on, let's go,' the policeman shouted, as he pushed his arm further up his back.

He started to sob, through pain or frustration I wasn't sure – probably both. 'Just let me see 'er ... five minutes, then I'll go wiv ya. I just *need* to see 'er,' he said, staring at me.

I looked at the officer. 'I'm happy to go in there and get it organised if it keeps him quiet. What d'you think?'

'I don't think the bugger deserves it, Mr

Cribb, but if it'll keep him quiet for the night I suppose it'll be worth it. Go on then. I'll wait with him here,' he said, still holding him in an armlock.

As I walked into the shop I thought about Uncle, who would've told him to 'sod off' until he'd learnt some manners and wouldn't have been remotely bothered that he was being taken away to the cells for the night. Maybe his way was right but I could see the bloke was desperate to see his mum and I couldn't turn him away.

I went to the chilled area and pulled his mother from one of the units, wheeling her into the Chapel of Rest. She was all prepared for the funeral, which was due to take place later that day.

I opened the door and walked back out. 'Come with me. You can see her now,' I said. The officer let him go. He stood there rubbing his arm. 'You've got ten minutes,' he said, as he followed me in. I showed him to the chapel, and he walked in as I closed the door behind me.

Exactly ten minutes later, the policeman returned. 'Where is he?' he asked.

'In there.' I pointed.

Opening the door he called out, 'Come on, time's up!'

He walked out and headed straight for the front door, not even looking at me. 'Hold on, hold on!' the officer said. 'We know you've forgotten your manners, but haven't you got *something* to say?'

He stopped, glanced around at me and muttered 'Fanks', sniffing and wiping his nose, before walking outside where the other officer was waiting.

'Unbelievable!' he said, shaking his head. 'He won't bother you again, Mr Cribb, and thanks for that.'

But I had an underlying feeling of unease that he would be bothering me again. I locked up and headed home. What an un-savoury character he was! I didn't know him from Adam, but, as I said, I didn't like him.

The following morning I arrived early at the premises and called Mrs Pryce's daughter. I explained to her what had happened and she was astounded.

'WHAT?' she screamed down the phone. 'I don't believe it! We never in a million years expected him to come back. He's got a bloody nerve! Did he mention the funeral?' she said, concerned.

'Well, he knows it's today, but he never said if he was coming or not,' I explained.

'What *did* he say?' she asked.

'Not a lot actually, he'd had a drink...'

'Oh, there's a shock!' she responded sarcastically.

I carried on. 'He just kept insisting on see-ing his mum as he hadn't seen her for years.

He was very agitated.'

'I bet he was. Probably needed another fix. He's always been into trying new drugs. He robbed Mum of all her savings so he could pay for his disgusting habit; cleared off to God knows where and none of us have heard from him for over fifteen years. He's an actor and a complete fantasist ... always has been. Listen, Mr Cribb, if he does happen to turn up and speaks to you, don't believe a word he tells you. He's a lying bastard who can't be trusted. If you don't believe me ask anybody who's there – they'll tell you the same.'

Although I believed every word she said, I didn't tell her what I had witnessed the previous night, as I was starting to feel uncomfortable. Getting involved in family disputes is never a good thing. Uncle's words of wisdom came back to me: 'Funerals bring out the worse in families, boy; underlying animosities tend to rear their ugly heads at times like these, so avoid them! Don't get involved, you're there to do a job, always remain impartial like the United Nations.'

There was an awkward pause. I had to say something: 'I can understand why you feel as you do.'

'Thank you,' she responded.

'Look, I'd better be off. You must have a lot to do. I'll see you later this afternoon at three.' I'd cut her short, but I didn't know what else to say.

That was it until later that day. Fortunately the weather had brightened up, as the rain had been torrential that morning.

When the cortège reached the cemetery there, leaning against the gates, smoking a cigarette, was the brother, still in the same scruffy clothes he'd had on the night before. I heard a groan go through the relatives sitting behind me.

Oh, sod it … here we go, I thought.

He followed in, trailing well behind the rest of the mourners, and sat on his own at the back. Nobody took a blind bit of notice of him. It felt like they were closing ranks to keep him out. There was an atmosphere of concern, as if they were waiting for him to start something but if he noticed he didn't show it – the only evidence that he was actually there was loud sniffing echoing around the chapel during the service.

When the coffin was taken outside for the burial, we all gathered around the graveside. He, for whatever reason, decided to stand next to me. I suppose because I always stood away from the rest of the mourners.

As the service commenced I saw out of the corner of my eye that he was staring intently down at the coffin. He turned his head towards me and whispered something. A whiff of whisky fumes hit me.

'Pardon?' I said, leaning across.

'I said, I wanna go wiv 'er.'

'What?'

'I wanna jump on top of the coffin and be buried wiv 'er,' he explained, still whispering.

I looked up in the direction of his sister; she too was staring at me. I then noticed that the entire group of mourners was staring at us. They'd been watching him and could see that he'd started talking. She gently shook her head and frowned. It was obvious she meant that whatever he was saying to take no notice.

I lowered my eyes again, then saw his feet edge forward. 'I'm going in,' he said.

'Go on, then,' I said, under my breath.

'*What* did ya say?' he said, his eyes spinning towards me in shock.

'I said, go on then.'

'Did you actually hear what I said?' he whined. 'I said I wanted to jump in and be buried wiv 'er.' He repeated it, slightly louder this time, his steps edging ever closer to the graveside.

'I know. I'm not deaf, I heard you the first time.'

'And you said, "Go on, then," he said, with an incredulous tone.

'That's right. If you want to go with her, then go.' I nodded towards the open grave. 'Go on, jump. Don't keep on about it, just bloody do it!' I was talking out of the corner of my mouth. I must have looked like a bad ventriloquist.

With that he turns sharply, looking directly at me. 'Well you're an 'ard bastard, aren't ya!' he shouted. 'I won't get any fucking sympathy from you, will I?' With that he made a lunge towards me but, due to the heavy rain, the ground was slippery, causing him to lose his footing. Within the blink of an eye he had gone. It was a terrible moment.

There was a sharp intake of breath from the mourners. They all stepped forward, peering into the hole, and there he was, flat out, lying on his back on top of the coffin. I saw his sister quickly raise her hand to her mouth. I thought she was going to burst into tears but she started to laugh, which then spread to the entire group. Me and the vicar were the only ones not laughing. This revolting man's behaviour had in my eyes defiled his mother's grave by his stupid antics. He quickly stood up on top of the coffin and was scrabbling at the side walls trying to get out. I bent down to offer my hand but his sister called out, 'I'd be tempted to leave him down there, Mr Cribb.' And then another voice joined in with, 'Fill it in!'

I ignored the jibes and managed to grab his hand, yanking him out. He flopped in front of me like a new-born calf but he was quickly on his feet. He was livid. 'You can all fuck off!' he shouted, which then made them laugh even harder, until he pushed me to one side and stormed off in the direction of the gates.

The mourners instantly began talking animatedly to each other. I walked over to his sister and asked to have a word. As we moved away from the rest of the crowd, I apologized. 'Mr Cribb, you have absolutely nothing to apologise for. You know what? I think that was Mum who pushed him in, or even my dear old dad getting his own back on him for doing what he did to her, but she had such a wonderful sense of humour, she would laugh at anything, and if she'd have been here she would've laughed at the aggravating little creep too. Everybody's been on their guard; it was inevitable he would try to cause merry hell sooner or later.' She put her hand on my arm. 'Come on,' she smiled. 'Let's get back home and we can have a toast to Mum, she'd like that.'

Back at the house the topic obviously returned to the brother. 'Hopefully the only damage done today was to your brother's pride,' I suggested.

'Pride! He wouldn't know the meaning of the word,' one of the uncles said angrily. 'Waste of space. Always has been, always will be.'

'He's right, Mr Cribb,' his sister chipped in. 'Ever since he left school, he's never worked ... thought it was above him ... God knows why! All he did was ponce off my mum, and she put up with it to save any aggravation. Then blow me down he goes and robs her of her entire savings. He hasn't an ounce of decency in him. A parasite, that's what he is – a bloody rotten parasite, and let's hope he stays away for good this time.'

'I'll drink to that,' said the uncle, raising his glass, to be joined by everyone else. I thought of what my uncle had said about the United Nations and decided this was a good time to make my exit.

Well, it was certainly a funeral to remember ... or maybe forget, and not one I would like to repeat.

That was the first and last time I'd been in a position like that, but this situation was unlike any other. He had, after all, tried to break into my premises. It was a one-off, like Mrs Vale, and fortunately would never happen to me again.

15

Eliza Joy
1964 (age 36)

As I answered the phone, and before I even had time to speak, an anxious woman's voice asked, 'Tom?'

'No, it's Stan, his nephew, who's calling please?'

'Oh, hello, Stan. I'm so sorry. I thought Tom would pick the phone up. I've not spoken to you before. I'm Eliza Joy. Your uncle has carried out quite a number of funerals for me over the years and sadly, I've had another bereavement, a beloved family member ... died yesterday after a long illness.' Her voice started to quiver.

'I'm very sorry to hear that, Mrs Joy. Uncle Tom is out at the moment. Would you like me to come round to sort the arrangements out for you, or would you rather wait for him?' I asked.

'No, that's fine, Stan. I'm quite happy for you to come round. It would be lovely to meet you. I'm in Clarence Road. What time should I expect you?'

'I'll be there within the hour. I'll see you

soon.' I hung up and was just getting my jacket on when Uncle walked in.

He sat down and lit up a Woodbine. 'Where you off to?'

'Eliza Joy called. A family member's died and she wants to sort out the arrangements, but she said it was OK if I went.'

'Eliza Joy? I've known her for years, lovely woman. She's had her fair share of losses. During the time you were away on military service she lost her mother, father and husband within the space of two years. She's got a brother, so it's probably him.' He took a deep puff of his cigarette and leant back into his chair, gently exhaling the smoke. 'I've always had a soft spot for her, you know.'

'What! I didn't think you'd have a soft spot for anything besides your prized roses,' I said incredulously.

'Well, there's a lot you don't know about me, boy! And don't start getting lippy. Now clear off! Don't keep her waiting,' he shouted.

'Well, now I know that, perhaps you'd like to go?' I started to say.

'Sod off!' he shouted, throwing a tin of polish towards me.

I dodged the polish and left. I walked around to see her, as it wasn't very far, and on the way I thought about what Uncle had said. I found myself smiling. It just goes to show, you work with someone day in and day out and you still don't know them.

As I approached the house I saw her anxiously peeking through the curtains. The front door was opened immediately by a lady in her late fifties, who had clearly been very beautiful in her heyday. Her once blonde hair was now streaked with grey and was swept up in a very fashionable 'chignon' (that's what Joan told me it was called. I would just call it a fancy bun) and she was very smartly dressed.

'Good afternoon, Mrs Joy, I'm Stan,' I said, offering her my hand.

As she took my introduction she said, 'Oh, I can see the resemblance with your uncle. Fine figure of a man he is, and so charming!' she said coyly. 'Come in, come in.'

I could think of a lot of adjectives that would fit the bill but 'charming' wasn't one of them. So many women used to say that about him; shame they didn't work with the miserable old bugger; that would've shattered their illusions.

She led me into her delightful little sitting room, and pointed to an armchair. 'Please sit down. May I offer you a small sherry, or maybe you would prefer tea? If it helps you to decide, I'm having a sherry,' she added.

'In that case, it would be rude of me not to join you, wouldn't it?' I said, smiling.

'It would indeed!' she replied warmly, as

she went over to her drinks cabinet and poured two Bristol Cream sherries. As we drank, she talked about all sorts of subjects, from the weather to the economy.

She continued for quite some time, then paused. 'Oh, Stan, hark at me wittering on! You don't want to sit chatting to me all day. I suppose we should get on with business.'

She hesitated, and I could see she was trying to compose herself.

'I told you on the phone that Bertie had died last night. I knew he was very ill, but you always think where there's life there's hope, don't you,' she said sadly.

'Yes, of course you do, and miracles do sometimes happen,' I said sympathetically.

'Yes, you do hear about things like that, but it wasn't to be. I don't know how I'll go on without him.' She stopped to wipe her eyes and blow her nose.

'Take your time, Mrs Joy, there's no rush. It's obviously a very difficult time for you.'

'You're very kind, Stan. Thank you for being so understanding. You see, since I lost my mother, father and my darling husband, Auguste, we've been constant companions to each other. I'd like to show him how much I ... love him by giving him the best send-off I can,' she explained.

'Of course, and you know that we're here to fulfil your wishes. How do you feel? Are you ready? As I said, there's absolutely no rush.'

'No, no. I'm ready as I'll ever be. We should get started,' she said, biting her lip, as she twisted her handkerchief in her hands.

'Shall we start with the casket? As you're aware, we make them from elm or oak.'

'I would like the elm, as it's lighter and I think he'd like that. Oh, and I would like the ruffles to be inside,' she said.

'Yes, of course, what colour would you like? Purple perhaps?' I suggested.

'Oh no, that's far too dark!' she said. 'I'd like the palest of blues, could you do that?'

'Yes, pale blue's not a problem. We'd normally use this for babies and small children, but if that's what you'd prefer,' I said as I wrote down the details. 'Have you a vicar or priest you'd like to conduct the service?' I asked.

'Funnily enough, I spoke to Father Goose this morning – he's an old family friend – and he's quite happy to do it,' she said.

'Excellent! He's wonderful; we use him a lot for our services. Now will it be burial or cremation?'

'Oh, definitely a burial,' she said.

'Lastly, how many cars will you require?'

'Only the one; there aren't many of us left,' she said wistfully.

'OK. I think I have virtually everything I need. I assume Bertie is at the hospital. Could you tell me which one, so we can collect him for you?'

281

'Hospital! No, no, he's not in a hospital, Stan, he's here. He died at home,' she said, looking surprised.

'Oh, my apologies,' I said. 'I just assumed ... so he's upstairs in bed, is he?'

'No, no, he's right here by my side where he's always been.' And with that she leant over the side of her armchair and lifted a blanket off the floor. 'Here's Bertie,' she said.

I couldn't believe it! There, lying dead on its bed, was a Pekinese dog.

She looked back at me. 'You look shocked, Stan. You do conduct funerals for animals, don't you?' she asked questioningly.

'Yes. Yes, of course we do,' I stuttered.

'Oh, I just knew you would! That's made me so happy. I can't thank you enough.' It was the first time I'd seen her smile. It was a lovely smile, and I could understand why Uncle had become smitten.

'Would you like me to take him with me now?'

'Oh, yes please, and could you bring him back tomorrow in his casket? Will you be able to make it in time?' she asked, concerned.

'No problem,' I responded. 'Tomorrow it is!'

'One other thing,' she said, getting up and walking outside.

When she returned she was holding a box, and in the box was a blanket, brush, several toys, a photo of herself and Bertie in a frame and a paper scroll tied with a blue ribbon. 'I would like you to place these in his casket, if it's not a problem,' she said.

'Of course, but I think I'll have to return to the shop and pick up our van so I can come back to collect Bertie and his things,' I explained.

'Oh, Stan, I'm sorry. I should have told you on the telephone. Then you could have come prepared. I've misled you, haven't I? You thought it was a person I was calling about, didn't you? I realised when you mentioned picking them up from hospital. Please forgive me for not having told you before,' she said.

'Absolutely not a problem. I won't lie to you ... I did think it was a person I was here to see you about, but everything's fine. No need to apologise. I'll head off now and be back within the hour.' And with that I left to pick up the van. I popped in to tell Tom what had happened. We'd never buried an animal before and I wasn't sure what his response would be, so I thought it best if I checked first.

'How'd it go, boy? Was it her brother?'

'No, it was Bertie?' I said.

'BERTIE? But Bertie's her dog!' he said, looking confused.

'I know. She wants us to bury him,' I said.

I was trying to stop myself grinning, as his face was an absolute picture.

'WHAT! Bury the dog?' he spluttered. 'Christ Almighty,' he said, scratching his head. 'This'll be a first ... for me anyway. Your grandfather only buried one in his time. I remember him coming home and telling us he'd taken it to the Pet Cemetery at Victoria Gate in Hyde Park.'

'I didn't know there was one there; I only know of the one in Ilford. When was it opened?'

'I think it was around 1880–81, around the time Father opened the shop,' he said. 'Prince George, the Duke of Cambridge, was the Ranger of the Park. By all accounts he was a colourful soul; was married to some actress or other. When her dog Prince died, he used his position and told the gatekeeper to give the dog a decent burial in the garden of his lodge. Course, once this was discovered all the society circles jumped on the bandwagon and wanted their pets buried there too.'

'Perhaps she'll want Bertie to be taken there,' I said. 'Is it still open?'

'No, don't think so. But what do you mean, *perhaps* she'll want the dog taken there, haven't you asked?'

'I forgot ... it threw me when I saw it was a dog,' I said, waiting for the barrage.

'You forgot to ask?' he yelled. 'What've you been doing round there? I bet you've been enjoying yourself, having cups of tea and a nice chat, haven't you?'

'We had Bristol Cream sherry actually,' I answered.

'Sherry ... bloody hell, it gets worse! But how in heaven's name can you *forget* basic questions like that? You've been doing it long enough!' He stood there shaking his head, muttering *'sodding Bristol Cream'* under his breath. He then looked back at me. 'How many cars has she ordered?'

'Only one,' I said.

'She knows that the dog can't be taken in the hearse, doesn't she?'

'Oh no, I didn't think of that either!' I said, horrified.

'Sounds like you didn't think of a lot of things. Well, you'd better make it clear when you go back. Explain it would be unethical but he can go with her in the car. Get around there now and get it sorted out and do it properly this time.'

After being screamed at again – truthfully after nearly twenty years I had got used to it – I got in the van and headed back. There she was at her window again, and had opened the door before I'd even got out.

As I walked in I said, 'If you don't mind, Mrs Joy, I just need to clear a few points up.'

'Is there a problem? Have you changed your mind about burying Bertie?'

'No, not at all. I just need to know where he's being laid to rest.'

'Oh, yes, we didn't discuss that, did we? It's a plot in the Ilford PDSA Pet Cemetery.'

'I know the one, that's fine. You also mentioned one car. Normally when we discuss cars the hearse is obviously included to carry the casket, but in this case I'm afraid we'll not be able to take Bertie in the hearse. He'll have to be put in the car with you and the other mourners. Is that OK?'

'Of course it is. I perfectly understand. It wouldn't be right, would it? There'll be plenty of room, as it will only be myself, my brother and his wife. My niece was going to come but she has another appointment,' she explained.

'Well, that's fine then. I'm glad we've got everything sorted out and you're happy. When would you like the funeral to be held?'

'Could we do it sooner rather than later? If you bring him home for the night tomorrow, could we do it on Wednesday? Would that be too quick?'

'No, Wednesday's fine. I shall drive you myself.' I smiled.

'That would be wonderful, thank you, Stan.' She smiled back. Uncle was right. She was a lovely lady.

'I'll be on my way now,' I said, as I bent down to lift up the basket containing Bertie. She was in tears. She stroked him, and said, 'Goodbye, precious boy. I'll see you tomorrow.'

I carried him to the van while she stood watching me from the doorway. She looked so sad. I did feel for her.

After taking him down to the workshop, to let Jack see what size casket he would have to make, I thought I'd pop along to see Father Goose and have a word with him about Wednesday, and see if he wanted to travel with us to the cemetery.

As I said before, Father Goose was a wonderful man. He'd been around our parish for many years, and during the war helped so many people through the Blitz. He also spent a lot of time helping at the boy's mission, where homeless boys were housed. He was always cheerful and positive. In fact, he was a pleasure to spend time with.

As I parked nearby, I saw him standing outside the parish church, with Reg, his assistant, although he was more like an adopted son. Poor Reg had been thrown onto the streets as a small child. He had a crippled leg and an unfortunate speech impediment, due to having no roof to the top of his mouth.

I could see they were talking, but couldn't hear what they were saying. As I got closer, I saw written on the church wall in large whitewashed letters: 'Father Goose is a Prick'. How on earth could anyone write that about him? I couldn't understand. There were lots of people who it could refer to, but he certainly wasn't one of them.

'Hello, dear chap, how are you today?' said Father Goose, smiling.

'That's a disgrace, Father!' I said angrily, pointing to the wall.

'I know, I know, Stan, but what can you do?' he said, shaking his head. 'But, do you know what ... they're not wrong, as I think I can be sometimes!' he said, having a laugh about it.

We then had a brief chat about Bertie and he was more than happy to travel with us in the car, so everything was fine.

Jack made the casket that afternoon. I polished it and fitted the ruffles the following morning in the rear of the shop, as I thought it would attract too many questions if I did it in the front window.

Before I placed Bertie in the casket I groomed him with his brush, placed his blanket at the bottom and laid him on top, putting his toys around him and the picture propped up by his head. I picked up the scroll to put between his paws, but as I was holding it I had an uncontrollable urge to read it. I thought it would be a poem but it wasn't, it was a letter.

My Precious Boy,

I cannot believe you are gone. How lucky I was to have had you with me for so many wonderful years and how I shall miss seeing your lovely face every day when you run up to greet me when I awake or when I come back from shopping. I always loved that. You filled my empty heart and house with so much joy. You always managed to put a smile on my face, even when I thought I would never smile again.

You have been there through my worst days, helping me through the darkness into the light with your constant friendship and love. I shall miss your little paw on my arm and your beautiful eyes longing me to feel better.

Thank you for bringing such happiness into my life. You shall live in my heart until we are together again. I will cherish the day when I shall meet you and Daddy at the gates of Heaven. It consoles me to know that you two are together again.

All my love,
Your Mummy x

I rolled it back up and slipped the ribbon back on. I stood there for a few minutes, thinking about what I had just read. Some people who aren't animal lovers have no concept of the loss experienced when a family pet dies. How it can release feelings as powerful as when a human being dies. They're never able to comprehend how a person can grieve so deeply for an animal and, more often than not, ridicule them.

I took Bertie back that afternoon. Mrs Joy had cleared the sideboard and asked me to place him on top. She looked down at him, her handkerchief held up to her face. 'I'm going to miss him so much.'

I placed my hand on her shoulder. 'At least you have your memories,' I said.

She looked at me sadly. 'Do you know, Stan, after the losses I've had, I sometimes wish I didn't have any. I know it sounds strange, but memories unfortunately do not bring me happiness. They bring me sorrow. Sorrow for what I have lost and will never have again. How I wish I could gain comfort in them as some people do. I do envy them. You know, more often than not I'll sit here and think of the wonderful times I spent with my mother, father and husband, and of course Bertie, and as I look back on those lovely days instead of smiling I'll cry. Sometimes I'll cry so much I think I'll never stop. But then I'll think, if I didn't have them what would I have? Life is a conundrum!' She looked back at me. 'You know, I've also thought, what if a doctor told me he could wipe my memory clean. What would my answer be? By the way I'm talking, it should be "yes", but I wouldn't hesitate in saying "no", because, for all the pain they bring me, what would it show if I didn't have them?'

'A dull, boring, unfulfilled life,' I answered.

'Exactly!' she said. 'I've discovered that happiness and sorrow are eventual bedfellows, and the sorrow in my latter years sadly outweighs the happiness. But I suppose, as the saying goes, "That's life." ' And with that she let out a deep sigh.

What could I say? I fully understood what she was saying, and trying to talk her round would be pointless, so we just stood in silence for a while.

'Well, I didn't expect to get into such a deep conversation,' she said a few minutes later. 'This is all you need, isn't it? I must sound like a batty old woman!'

'Not at all, Mrs Joy, I completely understand what you're saying.'

'Thank you, dear,' she smiled, putting her hand on my arm. As she looked back at Bertie she said quietly. 'He looks lovely, Stan. The casket and everything is perfect and I love the way you've placed the scroll between his paws. Thank you so very much,' she said, looking at me through her tears.

'I'm glad everything's how you wanted it. I'll leave you now and see you again tomorrow at eleven.'

'Yes, yes, see you tomorrow,' she said, as she turned back to look at Bertie.

I once again placed my hand on her shoulder. 'Stay there. I'll see myself out,' I said and then left.

The next day, her brother and sister-in-law were at the house, ready to go. They sat in the rear of the car and Mrs Joy sat in the front with Bertie by her side, where he'd always been, with her hand resting on the top of his casket.

The short service was held around the graveside, conducted by Father Goose. A headstone had already been carved and was ready to be set.

It read:

BERTIE

3.5.48–12.7.64
My beloved friend and companion

If tears could build a stairway,
And memories a lane
I'd walk right up to heaven
To bring you back again.

I'd seen this epitaph on quite a number of occasions over the years and it never failed to bring a tear to my eye.

As we turned to walk back to the car, I noticed another one had drawn up about thirty yards away. I didn't take much notice, as I thought it was somebody visiting another grave.

Out of the car climbs a young woman around twenty years old, and she's carrying something. Mrs Joy's brother whispers something into her ear and she looks up towards the young woman and smiles. 'Oh, Amelia, you managed to make it. How lovely of you. It's my niece, Stan,' she said.

Amelia walked up to her aunt. 'Hello, Auntie, I've got a surprise for you. Bertie thought that you might be lonely and asked me to give you this,' she said, handing out a bundle. As the blanket fell away, poking its head out was a tiny Pekinese puppy.

Mrs Joy let out a gasp. 'Oh, Amelia! How kind of you, how ... thoughtful! But I can't ... I just can't take it ... not now. I would feel as if I was betraying Bertie – that he could be replaced so easily.' She then started to cry.

'Oh, please don't cry, Auntie. I just thought that... I'm *so* sorry,' she trailed off, looking helpless and embarrassed.

'No, *I'm* sorry, Amelia. I know you only did it with the best of intentions, but Bertie to me was ... irreplaceable,' she said, wiping her eyes.

I stood listening to the conversation going back and forwards. I could understand how she felt, having just buried Bertie. I thought it best not to get involved, though, so I let them sort it out between themselves.

The puppy was eventually handed back to Amelia, who climbed back into her car and Father Goose, Mrs Joy, her brother and wife climbed back in with me. I then took them home. All the while the conversation was about Amelia and the puppy. It was decided that her brother would take it home and they'd keep it for themselves.

It was around four months later. I was walking along Rathbone Street when I saw her looking through the butcher's shop window, and next to her was a young Pekinese. It had a pink collar and lead and looked delightful.

'Good morning, Mrs Joy. How lovely to see you again, and who may I ask is this lovely little girl?' I said, as I bent down to pat her.

'Oh, Stan, how wonderful to see you too. This is Alberta. She's the puppy Amelia brought to the cemetery the day we buried Bertie. As you know, I couldn't take her that day, as I felt as if I would be betraying him. I've been visiting my brother regularly and he's been coming around to my house and of course I've been spending a lot of time with the puppy. Well, one day he says to me out of the blue, "Eliza, why don't you just take the puppy home with you. Bertie knows you loved him and he'd never want you to be at home all on your own. It doesn't mean you've forgotten about him or betrayed him. *Please* take her with you now." So I did! I thought, he's right, Bertie wouldn't want to see me alone and sad. So, here we both are. She *is* lovely, isn't she?' she laughed.

'She certainly is! You're both very lucky to have each other,' I said and smiled.

'I said when I first met you, Stan, that you resembled Tom, but now I know not only do you resemble him, you're as charming too.'

'Well, I'm lost for words! But thank you ... you're very kind,' I answered.

So I was as 'charming' as Uncle Tom. I didn't know whether to laugh or cry! When I got back to the shop, Uncle was sitting at his desk, engrossed in his newspaper.

'Come over here, boy,' he said, waving his hand at me.

'What is it?' I asked, as I pulled our dictionary off the shelf.

'Just come over here and look at this, will you,' he said, tapping his finger on a photo.

I glanced over his shoulder and there, on the front page, was the newly elected Prime Minister Harold Wilson.

'What do you see, boy?' he said, not taking his eyes off the photo.

'I don't know what you mean. What am I supposed to be looking for?'

'Just look ... look at his face and tell me what you see.' He was getting agitated, and I still didn't have a clue what he was on about.

'I don't see anything except a picture of a man,' I said unproductively.

'Exactly! Now that's the problem, boy, and that's what most people will see – just a man – but I want you to remember this moment.

There's an old saying that "If you put the Devil on a horse he will ride it to buggery" and that,' he said, tapping his finger on the photo, 'is exactly what's going to happen to this country. You mark my words. Anyway, what d'you need that dictionary for?' he asked, pulling it out of my hand.

'I just wanted to look up a word,' I said.

'No. Fancy that, using a dictionary to look up a word; who'd have thought of that. You silly sod, you amaze me sometimes, you really do. What's the word?'

'Charming,' I responded.

'Charming? You obviously know what it means; you're not that daft! Delightful, pleasant, charismatic, fascinating, polite, attractive, to name but a few. Why are you looking that up, for heaven's sake?' he said, looking at me in amazement.

'Well, Mrs Joy said before I left her just now that I not only resembled you, but I was as *charming* as well. I just wanted to double check that charming was what I actually thought it was, and she hadn't got the wrong word.' I waited for the barrage; I couldn't resist it.

'Eliza said you were as charming as *me?* That woman is one of the nicest, most intelligent women I've ever met. Now *she* optimises the word "charming".' He just sat there looking at me, strumming his fingers on the dictionary. 'You know what, boy, I think you're right this time ... she has got it wrong.'

I looked at him with wide eyes.

'In life we have to face up to some cruel truths and this is one of those times,' he sighed. 'It's an unfortunate fact of life, and we have to accept these things. The fact is, boy, no matter how hard you tried you could *never* be as charming as me.' He stood up, walked over to the shelf and replaced the dictionary, giving me a gentle squeeze on the shoulder as he passed.

What I have witnessed over the years is the way bereavement brings out so many different emotions in people. Each person deals with it in a completely different way: some want to talk about the person all the time and have photos around them, whereas others don't even want to mention their name. This seems foreign to some but, listen, if that's the way they deal with it, then let them do it. There are no set rules to bereavement; you deal with it in whatever way you can and, as Uncle Tom would say, if they don't like it, then 'sod 'em!'

Mrs Joy's Bertie was my one and only animal burial, and I often think what an enlightening experience it was. After conducting Bertie's funeral, and seeing Mrs Joy's grief at his loss, I'm mindful now when

I meet people who have lost beloved pets who have been constant friends and companions over many years. I now know their grief is as real as any other.

16

Uncle Tom
1972–1977 (age 44–49)

I was standing outside the office, sneaking a look through the glass panel, watching my wife and Uncle sitting by the desk. She had gone in there to help him with the books. I couldn't make out what they were saying but he was chain-smoking his Woodbines. This was never a good sign, as it always meant he was getting worked up.

The day before, he'd been in the office going over the books, cursing under his breath, when Joan had gone in to see if he was OK.

'Can I help you, Tom?' she asked.

'No,' he answered brusquely. 'You wouldn't understand. Just leave me alone!'

She walked away, looking over at me and rolling her eyes whilst I polished a coffin in the window.

I'd been going home to her virtually every night for the previous couple of months, getting increasingly stressed by Tom's behaviour. He'd become volatile, not physically but verbally. He'd always been impatient, as you well know, but over the past year or so I'd only have to put a tin of polish down in the wrong place and he'd have a go. It had been getting me down. I was at the end of my tether.

I also discovered that while I was out of the office visiting clients, 'walk-ins' or phone calls were either not being written down or written incorrectly, so I couldn't call them back. If I questioned him about it he would go berserk. I just didn't know what to do. The business was starting to suffer, as people who had called in were not being got back to, and the tension building up between us was becoming intolerable.

After discussing it with Joan, she offered to come and give me a hand while the children were at school. She would keep an eye on Tom when I was out and try to answer the phone before he did. It seemed like a good plan, but I would have to get him to accept Joan into the office.

Amazingly he was OK about it. Maybe he was secretly relieved that someone else was going to be there to give him a hand, but he would never have admitted it or asked for help.

The following day, after he'd told her she 'wouldn't understand', he headed back into the office to confront the books once again, but he was obviously still having trouble. Joan knocked on the door and, on the pretence of taking him a cup of tea, offered to help him once more.

'I told you, you *wouldn't* understand!'

'Well, why don't you explain to me what to do and I'll give it a try. Two heads are better than one, Tom; once this is sorted you can get on with something else.'

'Alright, alright, we'll give it a go,' he said reluctantly. 'Pull a chair up and I'll try to explain.'

They'd been in there around an hour when he slammed the accounts book shut, shouting, 'Oh, you're so sodding clever, aren't you! Well, you'd better take them home and do them yourself from now on.' He then pushed the chair away and stood up.

I turned and walked quickly back to my polishing. I didn't want him to know I'd been watching them, as he would kick off again. The office door was flung open and he stormed out, holding his overcoat and hat.

'I'm off!' he said, as he slammed the door.

'What on earth are we going to do?' Joan said.

'I've no idea,' I answered.

Would you believe that we carried on like that for nearly five years? It was tough, as during that period he tragically got worse and worse, and gradually stopped coming into the shop altogether. We now know he was suffering from Alzheimer's, but in those days it had never been heard of. We called it senility or senile dementia.

It was during this time that my sons Graham and John started to work with Joan and me. After leaving college they both decided that they wanted to join the business. I'd been slightly apprehensive about it, as you hear a lot about families having problems when they work together, but with Joan there to sort us all out it worked.

It was the early hours of the morning when the phone rang. I ran downstairs to answer it, thinking for the hundredth time that we must get an extension by the bed.

'Stan, it's Bert. Sorry to call you at this hour,' my uncle said apologetically.

'That's OK, what's happened?' I asked anxiously.

'Tom's gone missing,' Bert said, his voice shaky.

'Missing! What d'you mean, missing, what's happened?' I was still half-asleep and it wasn't registering.

'Well,' he continued, 'I heard a noise and thought it may have been a burglar, so I grabbed my walking stick and headed downstairs. Frightened the life out of me when I found the front door open, so I had a look around but there wasn't any sign of an intruder and nothing had been taken, so I locked the door.

It really shook me up. As I was going back to bed I thought I'd check on Tom, and when I looked in his room I saw he was gone. His clothes were still hanging behind the door, so he must still have his pyjamas on.' His voice had started to tremble.

I did feel for him. Poor Uncle Bert. As well as looking after Tom, who was now clearly in the grips of dementia, his wife of forty years, Lottie, was also suffering with it too, so he certainly had his hands full.

'I'll be right over,' I said. 'Have you called the police?'

'No, do you think I should?'

'Absolutely. Call them now and tell them what's happened, and I'll see you in twenty minutes or so. Don't worry, we'll find him; he couldn't have gone far.'

I quickly got dressed and headed over to their house in Leyton. The police were now out looking for him too. Uncle Bert decided he wouldn't come with me, as he was worried about leaving Lottie alone.

I drove around and around. I couldn't think where he would've gone. About half an hour later I saw a police car parked up at the roadside. I pulled in behind it.

The policeman was standing outside the car taking down some notes. I wound down the window and called out, 'Excuse me, I'm looking for my uncle. He's gone missing. He was only in his pyjamas. You haven't found him, have you?'

'I think we have,' the policeman answered, looking up from his notes. 'He's in the back.'

I got out and went up to the police car. I looked in the back and saw him sitting there, holding a cloth up to his head – it was covered in blood.

'What on earth's happened?' I said, turning to the policeman.

'We found him lying on the pavement. He'd fallen over and banged his head. We were just about to take him along to the hospital.'

'Has he said anything?'I asked.

'When we picked him up and sat him in the car he said he was looking for his horses, but there aren't horses round here,' he explained.

'No, I know,' I said. 'He's very confused. I'll have a word with him.'

I knelt down by the car door. He looked such a sorry sight.

'What you been up to?' I asked softly, placing my hand on his knee.

He turned his head and looked at me with such sorrow. 'I can't find the horses, boy, they're on their own, they'll need feeding and watering. I've got to find them, where *are* they?' He moved his legs, as if he was going to get out.

'Don't move, Uncle, just stay there, the horses are alright. I've just been to see them. They're fine, all fed and watered and looking forward to seeing you tomorrow.'

His eyes lit up. 'Really? They're *really* alright? I've been so worried about them.'

'I promise you they're fine. Let's just get you home, you can get some rest and you can see them tomorrow.'

'OK, boy,' he said, smiling.

I was overcome by sadness. I'd come to accept over these last few years that I'd been losing him, but at that moment I knew he was gone forever.

I turned back to the officer. 'I'll take him home.' And with that we moved him into my car. He never said a word on the way back.

Bert made him a sweet cup of tea and I cleaned him up and then we put him to bed.

'What are we going to do, Stan?' Bert asked anxiously when we were back in the living room. I knew he couldn't carry on like this for much longer.

'Don't worry, Uncle Bert, I'll sort something out,' I said. I then left him and went home to tell Joan what had happened.

Over the next few weeks it was decided between all of us that it would be better for everybody if Uncle was put into a home. He was becoming a danger to himself, as well as putting an enormous strain on Bert.

Joan, having been backwards and forwards to the doctors and Social Services, had secured him a place in Claybury Hospital in

Ilford. This was classified as a mental hospital.

'I don't want him to go in there. I can't do it!' I said angrily when she told me.

'Where else can he go, Stan? I've been sorting it out for weeks and there isn't anywhere else. I don't want him to go in there either but we've no option!'

I knew deep down she was right.

Nowadays there are all sorts of different homes where Alzheimer's sufferers can be admitted, but in our day they stayed at home or went into a mental hospital. We had no choice; we couldn't have him live with us. Now Joan worked in the business there was nobody at home to care for him and it wouldn't have been fair on her or the children – even though they were now grown up, they still lived with us at that time. So the decision was made – he would be admitted into Claybury.

Uncle Bert had packed his things. He didn't have much by then, just a small suitcase.

'Where we going, boy?' he asked, holding onto my arm as I led him to the car.

'Just for a drive, Uncle,' I said.

'That'll be nice,' he said, turning to me and smiling.

I drove around for a while, trying to prolong the inevitable. I wanted to talk to him but he just became confused, and when he was confused he became agitated.

We eventually pulled up at the hospital and I walked him in. It was only a short distance but strangely felt so far. I suddenly felt like a drowning man, my life flashing in front of my eyes. I had feelings of overwhelming betrayal, similar to the feelings I'd had when we took the horses to the Elephant and Castle.

How I wanted to save him! I would've done anything *absolutely anything* to stop him from going in there, but there was nothing on this earth I could do about it.

The nurse came out the front and welcomed us in. I got him settled into his room and then the time came when I had to leave him. 'I'll come back tomorrow, Uncle,' I said. I was distraught.

'See you then, boy,' he smiled, giving me a little wave.

My heart was breaking. How I walked away I don't know.

I went in to see him every day for the first few months, as I was so worried about him. He gradually settled into a routine and thankfully seemed very content. A nurse had befriended him and in his free time would sit and chat to him about the old days and the horses. Not our horses, but the original set my grandfather had kept, where Uncle had started out at twelve years old, like me, on the horses' hooves.

I was as happy as I could be. As long as he was content, then that was good enough for me. Ironically, soon after he was admitted, I was in the shop one afternoon when the door opened and a distinguished councillor who was well known in the area walked in.

'Hello, young Cribb,' he said.

Even though I was nearly fifty some people still called me 'young Cribb'.

'Hello, sir,' I answered. I walked over to him and offered my hand. He took it, shaking it vigorously.

'Everything to your satisfaction here?' he said, as he walked around inspecting everything. 'I must admit, it all looks lovely. They did a good job, didn't they? You must be so pleased with it. I'm surprised the old one didn't fall in on you!' he said, looking at me laughing.

Oh God, here it comes … all these years … Tom said this would happen. Thank goodness he's not here to see it. I couldn't even imagine what he would've done or said to this man if he'd seen him. I was wracking my brains thinking how much cash I had in the safe.

'We're thrilled with it, sir; they've done a fantastic job.'

There was a pause while he kept looking around.

'Is there something I can help you with?' I said.

'Yes, there certainly is,' he said, turning back towards me. 'Sadly my brother died this morning and I was hoping you could conduct his funeral.'

I nearly fainted.

'Of course, we'll be happy to sort it out for you.'

Not another word was mentioned about the shop and, after we had completed the arrangements for his brother, he stood up to leave.

'Before you go, would you mind if I asked you a question that has been puzzling my uncle and I for a number of years?' I said.

'Of course, what is it?'

'We could never work out why this new shop was built, and at no cost to ourselves.'

'Ahhh,' he said. 'I can easily answer that for you, as I vividly recall the meeting we had. When the papers came in front of the board for the old premises to be demolished and a request had been made for a new one to be built, all of the councillors had no hesitation in agreeing to pass it. You see, over the years most of us and our families have had dealings with either you, your uncle, and even your grandfather before that, so we decided un-animously that these premises would be built under the auspices of "service to the com-munity". Now does that answer your ques-tion?'

'Absolutely,' I said, smiling, shaking his

hand. 'Thank you *very much.*'

'No, thank you, young Cribb, thank you!' he said.

When he was gone I sat there. 'Services to the community' – so that was their reason for building it. I can't tell you how proud that made me feel.

The awful thing was, after I found out this wonderful piece of news I went straight in to see Uncle. I sat there excitedly telling him what had happened, and what the councillor had told me, but he had no idea what I was talking about; he just sat staring out of the window. That for me was the most heart-breaking part; he would never know why the new premises had been built. It would have filled him with joy to have known that.

For over a year I visited him weekly, even though he had reached the stage where he didn't even recognise me. It was shocking to see this once strong, quick-minded, exceptional man deteriorate in the way he did. The last time I saw him I was telling him about a funeral I had just conducted. Although he didn't respond, I knew he was listening.

'Would you like to organise another funeral, Uncle?' I asked, softly putting my hand on top of his.

'Yes,' he said, looking at me as a little spark came into his eyes.

I reached into my bag and pulled out an order form and pen and handed it to him.

'Here we are then,' I said.

He took it from me and scribbled over the page and then handed it back. 'There you go, boy, all done!' he said, smiling.

That was the last time I saw him. He died the next day, peacefully in his sleep. He was 86 years old.

My beloved mentor was gone.

I now had to arrange his funeral and I knew exactly what I had to do. Under normal circumstances only one undertaker is used, but in this instance I would be using two. I contacted Mr Tadman and Mr Rivett and asked them if they would conduct the funeral. They were the same undertakers Uncle had used for his own father's funeral, although it was now run by their sons. I was following in the family tradition.

Bill Whitehorn, our carpenter at that time, made the coffin. I polished it, then fitted the mouldings and handles. He had kept a specific set of handles for as long as I could remember, and occasionally would take them out to polish them, saying, 'Now don't forget, boy, these are to go on my coffin when the times comes.'

The funeral itself was very simple; he wouldn't have wanted anything else. We left from Bert's house in Leyton. Mr Tadman and Mr Rivett walked together at the head.

The service was held in Old St Luke's Church, in the presence of around 200 people. We had two services conducted by our old friends, Anglican Vicar Father Goose and Catholic Priest Father Hall. We used the two different denominations, as Uncle Tom had known these two men for many, many years, and liked and respected them both.

He was laid to rest with his father and mother in the East London Cemetery. For all of his cantankerous ways, I loved and missed him more than I could ever say.

17

They're Back
1984 (age 56)

We'd just sat down to one of my favourite dinners: calves' liver, bacon, mashed potatoes, onions and peas, topped off with a lovely thick gravy.

What more could a man ask for?

Then Graham pipes up: *'Please* come and look at the carriage, Dad.'

'Look,' I sighed. 'How many times do I have to tell you, I don't want to get involved with the carriages and horses!' I was getting fed up with his constant nagging over the previous few weeks, about a carriage he'd seen in a barn.

He was getting on my nerves.

'I just think it'll be good for the business to reintroduce the horses. You know they haven't been used since you were a boy and I've a feeling it's going to take off again,' he said, pushing another forkful of mash into his mouth.

'Here we go ... so now you're the H.G. Wells of undertaking, are you? Look, will you just forget it; I don't want to know!' I said.

Chronic indigestion was just around the corner.

I had slowly but surely turned into Uncle Tom.

After he'd left, Joan walked back in from the kitchen and sat down opposite me. 'Why don't you just go and look at the carriage? He's taken a lot of time searching for one he thinks would be right. I feel a bit sorry for him, doing all that work and all you keep doing is giving him knock-backs. He looked deflated when he left.'

'Look, Joan, it's not as if I've led him up the garden path. I told him I wasn't interested even before he started looking, so that's his bloody fault! You know what he's like, always thinking up "hare-brained" schemes. He's always been the same; he'll never change,' I answered.

'You just won't give in, will you? Just go with him, have a look, *then* tell him it's not the right carriage or something. Just let him see you've shown a bit of interest, otherwise it'll put him off suggesting anything else in the future, and you've got a short memory when it suits you!' she said angrily, heading back to the kitchen.

'Hang on ... what's that supposed to mean?' I asked.

She stopped and turned. 'Well, how many times did you come home complaining to me about how frustrated you got with Tom not wanting to listen to any of your ideas. You're doing *exactly* the same thing to Graham but you can't see it.'

Ding-ding end of Round 1. Hit with a killer blow, and not below the belt.

What she was saying was absolutely right, annoying but true.

'Alright, alright, I've got your point; I'll talk to him tomorrow.'

'Thank the Lord for that!' she said, disappearing into the kitchen.

The next week, there we were, heading off to a farm in the sticks to look at the carriage. When we arrived, Graham went off and had a chat with the farmer, who pointed us in the direction of the barn. It was ramshackle; in fact, it should've been condemned. Graham pushed the creaking double doors open, and inside it looked like a scene from Dickens. The sun shone through the gaps in the roof and walls, there were cobwebs everywhere and, tucked away in the corner surrounded by bales of straw, was the carriage. You could hardly see it for dust and birds' muck.

'I don't believe this! This hasn't seen the light of day since Queen Victoria came to the throne. I thought you said you'd seen it,' I said, walking up to it.

'Well, no ... I haven't actually seen it, Dad. Someone told me about it in the pub,' he replied, making sure not to catch my eye as he walked around to the other side.

'YOU HAVEN'T SEEN IT? I've come all this way to look at something you haven't even seen yourself! Don't you think I've got nothing else to do, boy?' I yelled.

'Everything all right in 'ere,' the farmer asked, looking around the door.

'Yes, yes, everything's fine. We're just discussing the carriage,' I lied.

'Oh, rightyho then, I'll leave you to it,' he said, pulling the doors closed behind him.

I lowered my voice. 'I only came because your mother was making me feel guilty, telling me you'd done a lot of work searching for the bloody thing, and now you tell me you heard about it in the pub!'

'Sorry, Dad. Mum must have misunderstood me,' he said, as he opened the carriage door and looked in.

'Misunderstood, my arse! It's obviously a get-up between the two of you,' I hissed.

By that time he was walking round the back, rubbing some of the dust and muck off.

'Well, it's London built,' I said.

'How do you know that?' he asked, as his head shot around the side gawping at me.

'By the style,' I answered. 'But there's no point in you looking around there. Here's where you need to look, to see if it's any good.' With that I bent down, wet my finger and started to rub along the wheel hub and there, to my surprise, it read 'Dottridges

Bros' who were one of the finest carriage-makers of their time. It did put a smile on my face when I saw it.

'What do you think?' Graham asked. He was getting excited.

'Let's get it outside in the daylight and have a proper look,' I said.

The farmer then arranged for a couple of his hands to pull it into the yard. He suggested we went inside for a cup of tea while they cleaned it up a bit.

After enjoying a nice pot of tea and some freshly baked cake we went outside to inspect the carriage. Well, it was a sight for sore eyes; it looked so much like our old carriage it brought an unexpected lump to my throat.

'Mmm, interesting. Needs a respray and quite a bit of restoring, but I think it *may* work. How much do you want for it?' I said, turning towards the farmer.

'£2,800,' he replied. 'That's a fine carriage, that is. You won't find many of them around these days.'

'Just a minute,' I said. 'I want a quick word with my son.' I then walked away with Graham, who looked like a Cheshire cat, and in a low voice I said, 'Look, this was your mad idea. If we get this you'll have to get it all sorted – the harness, horses, everything – don't expect me to be running around doing it.'

'I'll do it *all*, Dad. I promise you won't have to do anything,' he replied. He was thirty-two and he looked like he wanted to jump up and down like a kid. I had a flashback of Horace feeding Gracie the senna pods. I wanted to laugh, but couldn't with the farmer looking.

We walked back over. 'Right,' I said, '£2,000 for cash. I'm not into negotiating. You take it or leave it. It needs a lot of work done, which isn't going to come cheap, so that's the deal.'

I was expecting him to 'hum and haw' but he didn't. He just spat on his palm – and *I mean* spat on his palm, not that make-out spitting – held his hand out, and said, 'You've got yourself a carriage.'

I turned to Graham. 'Well, shake the farmer's hand, Graham; it *was* your idea, after all.'

He hesitantly held out his hand, and the farmer took it in a vice-like grip, pumping it up and down, saying, 'Pleasure doin' business with you gentlemen.'

Have you ever seen someone trying to smile but wearing a look of disgust at the same time? Well, that's how Graham looked.

As we were leaving he found an old water butt, plunged his hand into it and started scrubbing with his handkerchief. I had to walk off I was laughing so much.

The carriage was collected the next day

and, luckily enough, my son John had room to store it in his garage while we decided how this new-fangled scheme was going to work, or should I say until Graham had decided.

It had been sitting in the garage around a month and nothing seemed to be happening so it was time to have a word with H.G. Wells.

'I want to know what's going on with the carriage. It's been weeks since you carted me halfway round the country to spend £2,000 on that thing, and now it's sitting in John's doing nothing,' I said impatiently.

'I know, I know, I'm still trying to get a contact for the horses. I've got some information on a breeder but I'm having trouble tracking down his phone number,' he explained.

'I told you before, you're wasting your time looking for that breed. I bet they all died out when everybody changed over to cars forty years ago.'

'No, they haven't! I'm onto it and should know something soon,' he said.

Well, that was that – until a few weeks later when he came rushing in all excited again.

Now this was to start a course of events which you just won't believe...

'I've found someone!' he shouted. 'It's not the original man I was trying to find but through a fluke. Our neighbours' mother is visiting from Holland and she knows someone there who has three Friesians for sale,' he said breathlessly.

'So, what do you want me to do about it?' I asked.

'We've got to go over and see them *now* before she sells them to someone else,' he explained.

'Go over to Holland! Are you winding me up? This was your bloody idea, why have I got to troop over there too?'

'I just thought that you'd want to see them. After all, you are the *expert* on these horses, Dad.' He grinned.

I sighed. Although he was a pain in the arse, he certainly knew how to butter me up. 'When you planning on going, then?'

'This weekend. We can get the ferry over to the Hook of Holland and then hire a car to the woman's farm. John can come too,' he said, looking very pleased with himself.

'Alright, get it organised, we'll go and take a look. Might as well now we've got the carriage stuck there doing nothing.'

We left in the early hours of Friday morning. We drove to Harwich and picked up the ferry. It was a diabolical crossing – the sea was rough and none of us were particularly good sailors, so we were all the worse for wear when we got there. Having docked, we left the ship, happy to find our land legs again, although still feeling very delicate.

We hired a car and set off. The weather

was awful, teeming rain with a hurricane blowing. As well as not being good sailors, we were not particularly good map-readers either, and I can't tell you how many times we got lost. All we seemed to do was stop at petrol stations, asking for directions.

We drove for ages and it rained continually. I was *not* happy. What with the sea crossing and now this, I just hoped these horses were going to be worth the trip.

After nearly four hours we at last arrived at the farm, which was in the North of Holland in a place called Friesland. It is the only one of the twelve provinces of the Netherlands to have its own language, and where the breed of horses we were looking for originated from. Even though the weather didn't do it any favours, the farm didn't look much. It was very small and not the sort of place you would associate with a top breeder of horses. Something didn't seem right. I looked at Graham; he wouldn't look at me, as he was pretending to concentrate on the road. As we pulled up outside the farmhouse, I was even more concerned. It looked in a state of disrepair.

We all got out of the car and walked to the door. Graham knocked and it was opened by a lady in her mid-forties. She was very attractive, but looked as if she'd been experiencing tough times and didn't have the time or inclination to take care of herself anymore. She was puzzled when she saw us, and very politely said something I assume was in Frisian, the local language, but to be honest it was all double-Dutch to us.

Graham then said, 'Good afternoon, Madam, my name is Graham Harris. This is my father, Stan, and brother, John, and we have come from England to look at the horses you have for sale.'

'Horses?' she said in English. 'I haven't got any horses!'

With that, I shot a look at Graham, and, joking aside, I thought he was going to pass out. I saw him physically sway.

'No, Madam. You *definitely* have three Friesian horses for sale,' he said, speaking very slowly, as if she was simple or it would somehow make a difference to her answer.

'I am sorry, but I *definitely* haven't,' she said smiling.

'But you *must* have...'

'Are you not listening to the lady, Graham? She says she hasn't got any horses, and I think she'd know, don't you?' I said.

'But I don't understand.' Graham's voice was now quite pathetic. 'We've come all this way, as I was told that you had three horses for sale.'

'You'd better come in,' she said, leading us into a very cosy living room, with a roaring log fire.

'Let me make you a cup of tea and get you

something to eat and we can sort out where the confusion has come from.'

Off she went into her kitchen. I was sitting by the fireplace opposite Graham. I was still staring at him, but the little sod wouldn't look at me. He was fascinated by a pattern in the carpet.

John knew better. As I've previously mentioned, he'd learnt from a very young age to keep quiet and well out of it when his brother had dug himself into a hole. This was his brother's problem, not his, so he just sat there looking at the both of us.

Whilst we drank tea and ate a snack she had kindly made for us, she explained that she had kept horses in the past but after her husband had died a few years previously finances were tight, so she unfortunately had to sell them. How Graham had got news that she had horses for sale puzzled her.

We'd had the journey from hell and nothing to show for it, and now we had to turn round and go all the way back empty-handed.

'Just a minute. I think I *may* be able to help you,' she said, getting up.

Graham's head shot up so quickly I thought his neck was going to snap when she said this.

With that, she called someone on the phone and started writing down notes whilst talking in Frisian, so we had no idea what she was on about. When she hung up she turned to us smiling. 'That was a friend of mine who has contacts. He said that there's a farm around an hour from here, which does have a few Friesians, which he believes are for sale. He has given me the directions, so if you like you could try there. Hopefully something will come of it. I hate to think of you having a wasted journey.'

She then handed over the directions. Graham went and got the map out of the car and she marked the spot we had to head for. We thanked her for her hospitality, apologised for turning up out of the blue, and left.

We piled back into the car and headed off again. Nobody spoke; it was complete silence. Graham was in the back, and I knew he was just waiting for me to explode. He sat directly behind me with John in the driving seat. I think he was praying that as I couldn't see him I would somehow forget he was there.

I had just got myself geared up to turn around and give him a mouthful, when, fortunately for him, I saw a horse carrier ahead. As we got closer I saw it was carrying two black horses. We couldn't overtake but followed it for around four miles through country lanes. Finally the vehicle slowed down, indicating to turn into a side lane. As we passed it I looked down the lane and in the distance I could see some activity – there were lots of cars and horse boxes.

'John, turn the car around. Let's go and have a look at what's going on down there,' I said.

With that, we headed off down the path. At the end were several huge fields and those fields were full of Friesian horses. We had, by complete fluke, stumbled across a horse sale.

I glanced at Graham and had never seen a face look so relieved.

We parked the car and started to walk around. Graham had vanished, so it was just me and John looking at this beautiful display. They had grandparents, parents and foals, and it was wonderful to see them like that, generation after generation.

Over the loudspeaker the voice announced: 'Vill ze family of Cribb please go to ze main tent immediately.' Heaven only knows what type of accent that was. For a second I thought we'd travelled so far we had crossed over into Germany.

I turned to John. 'Christ, what the hell's the bugger gone and done now?'

We got to the tent and he's standing there with a man who looked like he'd stepped out of a John Wayne film, complete with ten-gallon hat, cowboy boots and one of those shirts with a metal buckle at the neck.

'Dad, you won't believe this,' he said,

turning to the cowboy. 'This is Bert Rankin. He's the man I was originally supposed to meet, and he's got some horses for sale,' Graham said gleefully.

'Good afternoon, gentlemen, welcome to Holland,' Bert said, shaking hands. 'Graham has explained everything to me, so if you would like to follow me back to my stables I can show you what I have.'

With that we jumped back in the car and followed him for about half an hour down the road. None of us spoke; I think we were all secretly hoping that at last we'd found someone who could help.

When we arrived he took us to a field that had five young horses walking around. They couldn't run, as it was like a bog. In fact they could just about lift up their hooves.

'We should get them out of there for you to have a proper look,' Bert suggested.

With that, Graham piped up. 'I'll get in. I'll round them up and head them to the gate.'

He started to climb over the wooden fence when his foot slipped on the top rung and down he went. It was a truly wonderful moment; he'd fallen face down into the field and was imbedded in the mud. I looked up to the heavens, smiling, thinking to myself that God certainly does pay debts in mysterious ways.

'That'll teach the little sod,' I said under

my breath.

After he had dislodged himself, and it took a while, as none of us offered to help him, he then managed to get the horses up to the gate where they were led into the stables.

'Now, I like that one there,' I said, pointing to the one at the rear. 'He's got a great presence.'

'You won't believe this, Stan, but he's the only one for sale. The rest are going to South Africa,' Bert said, smiling.

'The problem is we obviously need two, and if you only have one then I've got to find another from somewhere else,' I explained. I was thinking what a nightmare it would be to start looking again.

'I'll have him cleaned up for you and you can then have a proper look. If you would like to take a quick shower, Graham, I'm sure I can find you some clean clothes.'

I wanted to say, 'Leave the bugger as he is; won't do him any harm to make him suffer a bit more,' but I didn't. John and I left them to it and went to have a well-deserved cup of tea.

As Graham came back to meet us, we both simultaneously burst out laughing. Bert Rankin obviously didn't possess any normal clothes in his wardrobe and had decked Graham out in an outfit that Wild Bill Hickok would've been proud of.

Bert came in and told us the horse was

ready. He opened the stable doors and two beauties came trotting out, their heads held proud. They were picking up their hooves as any funeral horse should. They were perfect ... absolutely perfect.

'But you said you only had one?' I said, looking at Bert.

'It's his half-brother; a friend of mine had him up the road in his stables. I sent one of the boys up to collect him whilst we cleaned up the other one. What do you think, magnificent, aren't they?' he said proudly.

'They certainly are,' I said. 'How much?'

'£3,500 each but you can have the pair for £6,500,' he said.

Without hesitation I replied, 'We'll take them.'

Graham leaped up, punching the air. 'Yes!' he shouted.

The happiness on his face made me smile. We were at the start of a new era. I must admit I was starting to feel excited too.

Having had a journey over that we wanted to forget, coming back was far more enjoyable. The weather had brightened up and so had our spirits, knowing we had secured two lovely horses.

Graham's mood, having been extremely joyful, bizarrely changed when we left our hire car and made our way onto the ferry. It must have been down to the fact that not many people had seen 'Wild Bill Hickok' in the flesh, and he proved to be a great source of entertainment to the passengers as well as to me and John.

It took two weeks for us to receive the horses. Graham arranged for a horse carrier to go over and collect them (at least he got that right) and they were then taken to John's to be trained. These were young horses that had not been broken in, so it would take at least nine months to train them well enough to pull the carriage.

In the meantime the carriage was taken to George and Bert Scammell in West India Dock Road. They were 'master craftsman'-restorers of fine carriages. I'd shown them photos of grandfather's 1912 carriage. All funeral directors in the old days had their own colours. All the carriages were black but they were lined in a specific colour to show which business they belonged to. Ours were lined in blue with gold leaf filigree, so our new carriage would be restored in exactly the same way. Graham also had all the harnesses made. These were embossed with the initials 'TCS' – Thomas Cribb & Sons.

When everything was complete, the horses would be harnessed up and driven around the streets to get them familiar with traffic and any other distractions. This certainly caused a stir in the area. People would come out of their houses to watch them go by. It turned into quite a spectacle, as funeral horses hadn't been seen on the roads for many years.

After forty-one years, on 1 March 1985, our first horse-drawn funeral was held. I can't begin to explain to you how it felt after all those years.

The night before, I went into the office and pulled the ancient trunk out from the back of the cupboard. As I opened it, the smell of the old days came rushing back to me. I gently lifted out the 'velvets' and placed them on the table. As I unwrapped them, I'm not ashamed to say I had tears in my eyes. They looked as good as they had all those years before when I'd packed them up.

I sat down and thought about all the times that had long gone, and how Grandma and Uncle would have felt if they'd been there to see the horses back once again. They would have been so proud and I hoped they would've been proud of me too. Uncle had been my guide and teacher every step of the way throughout my life, and I was privileged to have been chosen as his 'apprentice'. How I missed him and those wonderful days.

The following morning I put the velvets in my car and took them along to where they were preparing the horses for that first day. As I started to fit them onto the harnesses I realised that the only difference was I didn't have to fetch a stool to stand on.

The activity surrounding them being prepared, feeling their warm bodies under my hands, and the smell and weight of the velvets, as I draped them down their sides, took me back.

I climbed up on top of the carriage, closing my eyes for a few seconds, trying to compose myself. It started to pull away and all I could hear was the sound of the horses' hooves on the roadway and the roll of the carriage beneath me.

My mind flashed back to my childhood. I was fourteen years old and it was the beginning of my apprenticeship. My beloved uncle was next to me and our beautiful horses were pulling us proudly along, their magnificent heads held high ... all of them long gone, but they will remain forever in my heart.

Th' hast spoken right, tis true,
The wheel is come full circle, I am here.

William Shakespeare *King Lear*

18

New Generation
2008 (age 80)

'Tell me about the horses again, *please*, Granddad,' Jack would say to me for the hundredth time. He loved listening to the stories that I've been telling you in my book.

He would sit for hours, his eyes growing larger and larger, as I told him about living through the war years when I was a young boy, showing him the old photo album of my grandfather's shop, and the original horses and carriages they had used.

'I want to be an undertaker when I grow up,' he would say eagerly.

'We'll see, son, you've got a long way to go before you have to start thinking about work. Just concentrate on your school work first,' I told him.

'But I *really* do, Granddad,' he insisted.

Graham would take him down to the stables at the weekends when he was a small boy, and he'd walk around with his bag of carrots and packet of mints, feeding the horses and screaming with laughter as their lips brushed over his little hand. He was as happy as a sandboy amongst them. I loved watching him; it reminded me of myself all those years back at our old stables when we used to go and visit Grandma and Uncle Tom, and what magical times they were.

As the years flew by, every now and again he would remind me of the fact that he still wanted to work in the business, which did make me happy.

The day came when Graham came into my office. 'Dad, you know Jack's leaving school in a couple of weeks. He still wants to come and work in the business – what d'you think?' he asked.

I had secretly hoped this day would come and now it had. 'Well, he's been on about it for long enough; it's obviously something he wants to try. Tell him to come and see me on Saturday at eleven,' I said coolly.

'OK, he'll be here. Thanks, Dad.'

As the clock struck eleven, Jack was knocking on my door. He was very punctual, which was certainly a good start.

'Come in, Jack,' I said.

'Good morning, Granddad.'

'Good morning, son. So, your dad's been telling me you're leaving school in a couple of weeks.'

'That's right. I can't wait!'

Oh, I know how you feel, boy.

'So you still want to work in the business?

You haven't changed your mind, then?' I asked.

'No, I've *never* thought about doing anything else, you know that. I've told you enough times!' he said, laughing.

I smiled. 'I know. I'm just checking. So what date do you finish?'

'Friday the 25th.'

'Right, I want you down the stables at 8 a.m. on the 26th,' I said.

'That's fantastic! Thank you *so* much. I won't let you down,' he said excitedly.

'You'd better not, boy. Now, off you go and I'll see you then,' I said dismissively. I didn't want to let on how pleased I was.

He virtually skipped out of the office.

On the 26th I arrived at the stables. I got there around 7 a.m., as you already know I love mornings. It was the start of a beautiful summer's day – the sun still low in the sky. I breathed the air deeply; the smell of the stables reached me. I would never tire of that smell.

I sat on the bench outside and rested my head against the wall. I closed my eyes, feeling the gentle warmth of the early sun. I could hear the horses inside.

Here I was waiting for my grandson to arrive and start out on hopefully his new career, as I had done sixty-six years previously ... sixty-six years! Where on earth had the time gone? How could that be ... it just didn't seem feasible.

When you're young and your parents, grandparents, aunties and uncles all say to you that *Time flies, you'll turn around and you'll be middle-aged,* you don't believe it for a second, do you? You think it's just old people talking ridiculously, that time can't possibly move that fast. How can your life fly by without you noticing? But believe me it does.

My thoughts went to my own dad, talking about the importance of a job with a pension. *'Son, you're young today but trust me when I tell you, and it'll happen quicker than you think, you'll turn around, and you'll be in your fifties, but it'll seem like only yesterday we were sitting having this conversation...'* How right he was. But it was far, far worse than he said it would be. I didn't turn around to find myself in my fifties. When I turned around I was in my seventies and within a blink of an eye I was eighty.

My daydreams were broken as I heard wheels on gravel. I opened my eyes and Jack was parking his car – how times had changed! He got out and walked towards me.

'Good morning,' he said smiling.

'Good morning, Jack. Sit down here a minute, will you. I just want a quick word with you before you get started,' I said.

As he sat down, I turned to him. 'Firstly I want you to know that I'm very happy you've decided to join the business.'

'Thanks, Granddad, so am I.' He smiled again.

'But you need to understand that this is a hard business. It's not physically demanding as it was in my day, but it's still emotionally very challenging,' I explained.

'Yes, I know,' he said, nodding.

I sighed.

'No, you *don't* know, Jack. It's impossible for you to know until you've done it.' He needed to understand the demands he would be facing.

'I'm sorry, I didn't mean...' he started to say.

'It's OK, but *listen* to me. I'll give you the same advice Uncle Tom gave to me when I started. And that is, you *must* treat every funeral as if it's your first. Do you understand?' I said.

'I think so,' he answered.

'Look, we're called undertakers for a reason. People have handed over their loved ones to us and we "undertake" to bury them with the utmost dignity and respect. Each funeral must be conducted in exactly the same way, whether you have one a day or six. *Now* do you understand?'

'Yes, now I do,' he said, nodding.

'Good! And this point is also *very* important. If you ever feel yourself becoming bored or complacent then it's time for you to move on and do something else, as neither the business nor I will tolerate it. Do you know why?' I asked.

He sat and thought for a while. 'Does it mean that if you feel like that then you won't be giving a hundred per cent, so your standards will drop?' he said apprehensively.

'Exactly right. If you don't give a hundred per cent *every day* and for *every funeral*, then the service and professionalism we have, and that we've aspired to for those years would be lost and that's completely unacceptable. This is like no other job. You're dealing on a day-to-day basis with people who are at their lowest. To bury a loved one is one of the hardest things they will ever have to do, so you must treat each and every one of them with kindness and compassion. This isn't a job where you can bring your troubles to work; they must be left indoors, no matter how fed up, angry or down in the dumps you feel. As soon as you walk through those office doors, you leave your problems behind until you walk out again. I can't emphasise enough how important this is.'

'I totally understand, Granddad, and I *promise* I won't let you down,' he said earnestly.

'OK, son,' I said, as I squeezed his knee. 'Now, let's get you started.' We both stood up and walked towards the stables.

Pete, our head coachman, was already at work.

'Pete?' I shouted from the door.

'Yes, Stan, here I am,' he called from behind one of the stalls. He then walked out to join us.

'Jack's here to start work. He's driven you mad enough in the past, although not as much as his father,' I said, as they both laughed. 'Show him the ropes, will you.'

'Course I will. D'you know where you want me start him?' he asked.

Oh, I know exactly where to start him, Pete.

'There's only one place and that's at the bottom. Let's start him on the horses' hooves,' I said.

'Right you are. Come with me, Jack,' he said, as they walked away.

I waited for them to go and then I turned away. The time felt right to hand the reins over to the next generation.

Postscript

I am enjoying my life in the Essex countryside. I retired from the company in 2008, but still play a very active role attending funerals. My wife Joan sadly died in 2001 and I remained alone for quite a number of years until meeting my lovely new wife, Lin.

Graham and John run the business together. Graham is normally found conducting funerals with his two sons: Jack, who you already know about, and Joe. John works on the administration/accounts side in the offices with his daughters, Sarah, Nicola and Katherine. Susan, my daughter, had a brief spell a year ago but left to start her family after she married an undertaker. They have two children, Claire and James.

I often think about Graham's idea to start up the horses again – perhaps he was the H.G. Wells of undertaking after all, as we now stable seventeen horses and these are out virtually every day.

From the one business that was set up by my grandfather, we now have fifteen shops over the Essex area and have been called out to conduct funerals all over the country. When Uncle Tom died, and the boys came to work for us, I believe that through hard work, the knowledge that was passed down to me and I passed on to them, combined with their youthful enthusiasm and the ideas they brought to the table, enabled us to achieve what we have today. It certainly wasn't easy, and it took many, many years of dedication from all of us, but the end result for me is hugely rewarding. It's more than I, and I'm sure Uncle and Grandma could have ever dreamed of. I know for sure that both of them would be flabbergasted to know that we have had a six-week fly-on-the-wall documentary made about us called *The Grave Trade,* which was shown on TV and, as a result of its success, a second series is being shown as I write.

We've also opened a large funeral home in Ghana. This was decided on after many Ghanaians who now live in the area wished for their loved ones who had passed away to be repatriated to their homeland.

I am also kept busy with my charities: The Horses' Trust, of which Princess Anne is the patron, and whom I've had the privilege to have met on several occasions at Buckingham Palace. This charity raises money for homeless and retired horses. I was also lucky enough to be invited in April 2014 to Highgrove by HRH Prince Charles for my services to the equine industry. The Prince is also the Patron of the Hackney Horse Society which, I'm very proud to say, recently approved me as President. There is also the Company of Farriers – they train up student farriers and are also very involved in the welfare of horses.

Lastly, but certainly not least, the Road Club of Horses and Carriages. There are around eighty members. We meet up once a year and take our carriages out and about around London and through the country to raise money for Help For Heroes.

I'm still a keen bird collector and have several aviaries in my garden, which house many rare types of birds, but unfortunately no chickens!

I hope that you have enjoyed reading my stories. I have certainly enjoyed relaying them to you. But I have one more to tell you before I go:

A few weeks ago, I was called in on the special request of an old customer. I had conducted around ten of her family's funerals over the years. I met her son to go through the arrangements. When we reached the point of choosing the casket he said to me, 'Mum made it clear to all of us that she specifically wanted you to carry her out from her home.'

'Yes, of course,' I replied. 'I'd be happy to be one of the coffin bearers.'

'No, you don't understand,' he said. 'She wanted you to carry her out.'

I smiled and said, 'I'm eighty-four. I can't carry a coffin out on my own. I wouldn't have been able to do that even when I was younger!'

'I'm sorry, Mr Cribb, but you still don't understand,' he said, getting embarrassed. 'Her actual words were: "I want Stan Cribb to carry me out to the hearse. Not in a coffin ... in his arms."'

Well, you could have knocked me down with a feather! I'm not often lost for words but I was then. I had to explain that unfortunately it couldn't be done – that his mother had to be placed in a casket – and I would be happy to be a bearer. He reluctantly agreed, although he wasn't very happy about it, but there wasn't an alternative – thank goodness – not at my age!

Stan Cribb, 2015

Acknowledgements

I was sitting watching the fireworks on New Year's Eve 2012 and, for some unknown reason, I had the sudden urge to write a book about Stan Cribb. I have known Stan for most of my life. My great-grandfather Marcus Rickwood was a good friend of Thomas Cribb, who was Stan's grandfather back in 1881. He was a sign-writer who painted the frontage of the original shop. They had thirteen children, and my grandmother, Eliza, was the eldest child. Mortality rates were very high in those days and having big families meant there would inevitably be more funerals. I came to meet Stan as he and Tom have conducted all of my family's funerals over the last fifty years.

I contacted his son John soon afterwards and arranged to go and see him at one of their funeral homes, in Beckton. Whilst I was there, he rang Stan and asked if he would be interested in writing his memoirs, which I'm happy to say he agreed to.

I went to see Stan at his lovely home in Essex, and we had a wonderful afternoon chatting and laughing about the old days whilst being fed and watered by his lovely wife Lin, who, by the way, makes the most delicious cakes! It was an absolute pleasure to go and see them every ten days or so and write down Stan's stories.

At first I was very apprehensive sitting in front of my laptop, getting out my notes and Dictaphone to start writing my very first book. Staring at that blank page that needs filling with words was a daunting experience, but then I heard Stan's boyhood voice talking and off I went.

I must admit, I found the entire process really enjoyable. My niece Katie, who is also a writer, suggested I read Stephen King's *On Writing,* which helped me enormously. He recommends that when you have finished the first draft, you should lock the book away for at least six weeks, and give the key to someone else, so you will not be tempted to go back to it. After this time has passed, make a large flask of your favourite drink, (after waiting all this time I was tempted to forget the flask and take a chilled bottle of Sauvignon, but I refrained) and go somewhere quiet and read the whole book from cover to cover. By doing this, any small discrepancies or spelling mistakes will 'jump out' at you. I did this, but it was really difficult not to look at it or do anything with it for such a long time, but his advice worked and I was pleased

I followed it.

Another suggestion he made was that once you had corrected your manuscript, print off four or five copies and ask your family or friends or someone you trust to read it, but they must tell you the truth and give you feedback. If one person mentions something they didn't like, take no notice, as it's just personal preference, but if they all say the same thing then you should change it. I did this and the feedback I received was so helpful that I ended up showing it to about twenty people over the next few months. The help they gave me was, I feel, invaluable.

That is where my acknowledgement comes in; it's for all the people who took the time to read my manuscript before I sent it to the publisher. Thank you, everyone ... the book just wouldn't have been the same without all of your suggestions.

Firstly Alex Montgomer – a friend and renowned journalist who read my book when I was just halfway through. I was losing my confidence and feeling it wasn't good enough to continue. He gave me the encouragement to finish.

Then, once finished, my Mum and Terry. My mum also was a great source of information regarding the Blitz, as she is a few years older than Stan and lived only two roads away.

I'd also like to thank the following: Mike Dunn, Katie Bazire-Smith, Carly Bazire, Zoki Kuzmancevic, Joe Pawlikowski, Louise Vyce, Rebecca Kisko, Jane Nottage, Cliff and Laurie Board, Myrtle Hockham, Bruce and Anna Walker, Paul and Lin Bazire, Tracey Graham, Suzie Bazire, and last, but definitely not least, Jeff Powell – another renowned journalist and good friend.

Yvette Venables, February 2015

The publishers hope that this book has given you enjoyable reading. Large Print Books are especially designed to be as easy to see and hold as possible. If you wish a complete list of our books please ask at your local library or write directly to:

Magna Large Print Books
Magna House, Long Preston,
Skipton, North Yorkshire.
BD23 4ND